Due Return	Due Return
Date Date	Date Date

The Valuation

of Nationalized Property

in International Law

Volume II

VIRGINIA LEGAL STUDIES *are sponsored by the School of Law of the University of Virginia for the publication of meritorious original works, symposia, and reprints in law and related fields. Titles previously published include:*

Central Power in the Australian Commonwealth—An Examination of the Growth of Commonwealth Power of the Australian Federation, by the Rt. Hon. Sir Robert Menzies, former Prime Minister of Australia, 153 pp. plus appendix and index, 1967.

Administrative Procedure in Government Agencies—Report by Committee Appointed by Attorney General at Request of President to Investigate Need for Procedural Reforms in Administrative Tribunals (1941), 121 pp. plus preface and index, paper or cloth, reprinted 1968.

The Road from Runnymede—Magna Carta and Constitutionalism in America, by A. E. Dick Howard, 382 pp. plus appendixes, table of cases, and index, 1968.

Non-Proliferation Treaty: Framework for Nuclear Arms Control—Ascertains the meaning of the Non-Proliferation Treaty and explores its potentialities in relation to the concrete problems which will be encountered as it is implemented, by Mason Willrich, 186 pp. plus appendixes and index, 1969.

The Legal Systems of Africa Series—Volumes published cover Ethiopia (by Kenneth R. Redden, 1968); French-speaking Africa south of the Sahara (by Jeswald W. Salacuse, 1969); and Congo-Kinshasa (by John Crabb, 1970).

Mass Production Justice and the Constitutional Ideal—Papers presented and proceedings of a conference on problems associated with the misdemeanor, held at Charlottesville April 10–12, 1969, under the sponsorship of the School of Law, in conjunction with the Sesquicentennial of the University, edited by Charles H. Whitebread, II, 222 pp. plus table of cases and index, 1970.

Education in the Professional Responsibilities of the Lawyer—Proceedings of the National Conference on Education in the Professional Responsibilities of the Lawyer, held at Boulder, Colorado, June 10–13, 1968, under the sponsorship of the Association of American Law Schools, edited by Donald T. Weckstein, 358 pp. plus annotated bibliography and index, 1970.

The Valuation of Nationalized Property in International Law—Essays on contemporary practice and suggested approaches by Dale R. Weigel and Burns H. Weston, Gillian White, Ignaz Seidl-Hohenveldern, Sir James Henry, Richard B. Lillich, Sidney Freidberg and Bert B. Lockwood, Jr., and Roger P. Smith, edited by Richard B. Lillich, 167 pp. plus index, 1972.

Legislative History: Research for the Interpretation of Laws—A listing of ideas and sources plus a description of routines useful in making a search for federal legislative history, by Gwendolyn B. Folsom, 132 pp. plus index, 1972.

The Valuation

of Nationalized Property

in International Law

Volume II

Richard B. Lillich

Editor and Contributor

The University Press of Virginia

Charlottesville

THE UNIVERSITY PRESS OF VIRGINIA
Copyright © 1973 by the Rector and Visitors
of the University of Virginia

First published 1973

ISBN: 0–8139–0465–X
Library of Congress Catalog Card Number: 70–177376
Printed in the United States of America

This volume may be cited as
2 THE VALUATION OF NATIONALIZED
PROPERTY IN INTERNATIONAL LAW
(R. Lillich ed. & contrib. 1973).

To

MARTIN DOMKE

International Lawyer

par excellence

Foreword

THE client's nagging question "How much money will I get?" not only goads the lawyer to be practical but also forces him to examine the theory of his case. A further volume of essays on the valuation of nationalized property in international law thus helps to maintain two sound disciplines for international lawyers who concern themselves with questions of nationalization of property.

The very fact that this and its predecessor volume concern themselves with the valuation of nationalized property confirms what is already abundantly clear—that an alien whose property is taken has no claim to restitution of his property in kind in the absence of special requirements under treaty or municipal law. The *Chorzów Factory Case,* so often resorted to as a source of wisdom on legal remedies for the taking of property, spoke of restitution in kind of nationalized property only because of the violation of a treaty, which had provided for the taking of property subject to compensation under certain defined circumstances. The taking of property dealt with in that case did not fall within the permissible category. And the judgment in the *Expropriated Religious Properties Case* called for restitution in kind of property in response to requirements laid down by the municipal law of the respondent state. There is, it can be asserted with some confidence, no adjudicated or arbitrated case in which restitution in kind of property has been ordered in the absence of a provision of a treaty or of municipal law which expressly or by implication calls for that action. The nature of the wrong done to the alien may thus be seen as not the taking itself but the failure to pay for the property taken at whatever standard of compensation is appropriate under the circumstances.

What that level of compensation is has been articulated in a variety of verbal formulae ranging from the mildly evocative to the operationally unmanageable. They are the standards under which armies fight, serving to identify differing ideologies, theories, demands, and defenses. In the familiar formula "prompt, adequate and effective compensation," the concepts of "prompt" and "effective" are difficult enough to elaborate, but the term "adequate," standing by itself, is only a feeble flame in the prevailing darkness. However, it is one of the conventions of international life that "adequate" is taken to represent a demand for "full" compensation or compensation in terms of "fair market value." But "fair" or "just" or "appropriate" offers no key to the measure of compensation to be provided, other than that it should be less than full and more than nothing. Valuation simply cannot be accomplished under any such opaque concepts.

"Prompt, adequate and effective compensation" and even the national treatment standard for aliens do at least direct attention to valuation, and thinking about valuation inevitably leads to consideration of the various elements which may or should be taken into account in determining the value of an alien's property. It is this breaking down of the problem into its component elements that is the principal contribution of this and its predecessor volume. The special understandings of the accountant, as reflected in Mr. McCosker's study of "Book Values in Nationalization Settlements," and of the economist, demonstrated in "An Economic Analysis of Aspects of International Expropriation of Property" by Professor Mintz, should be of material assistance to the lawyer in his analysis of problems of compensation. The rigor of their analysis should correspondingly discourage escape into empty verbal formulae by lawyers, academics, and diplomats.

The process of identification of the elements and criteria of value can be used not only to increase the compensation payable but also to provide a basis for its reduction. The valuation of property on the basis of book value, the employment of assessed value for the purpose of taxation, the subtraction of what are regarded to be excessive profits, the disapproval of debts not "usefully employed," the treatment of certain property as historically that of the state rather than of the alien are all means whereby a valuation paying lip service to full or adequate compensation may be brought down to the vanishing point. The adroitness of the Chilean government in finding means of reducing the compensation which would otherwise be payable on account of the nationalization of the business and properties of Sociedad Minera El Teniente, S.A., is a highly instructive example of the way in which the process of valuation can be employed to deny compensation. The legal position of the Kennecott Copper Corporation in its dispute with Chile, as set forth in Chapter V, is on that account deserving of particularly close attention.

The problems of valuation would not vanish but they would be simplified if there were a common, accepted standard for the payment of compensation for nationalized property. The provision on compensation in General Assembly Resolution 1803 (XVII) of 1962, the Declaration on Permanent Sovereignty over Natural Resources—that "the owner shall be paid appropriate compensation, in accordance with the rules in force in the state taking such measures in the exercise of its sovereignty and in accordance with international law"—papers over the fundamental source of disagreement between the developed and developing countries. The formal record of 87 votes, including that of the United States, in favor of the Resolution as against two votes in opposition and twelve abstentions indicates no more than the willingness of a large number of states to be content with an essentially ambiguous formulation, which speaks in the same breath of a national standard and an international one. Professor Bergin's felicitously expressed imaginary debate, which forms the first paper in this volume, shows the diversity of attitudes taken toward this question of compensation and the philosophical and ideological foundations for those attitudes. His own preference is clear, but he more than does justice to the views of those with whom he disagrees.

The situation is the more appalling if one attempts to determine the state of the law by reference to the sources of international law referred to in Article 38, paragraph 2, of the Statute of the International Court of Justice. Particular international conventions, to use the terminology of the Statute, do exist, but they reflect the bargains struck by pairs of treaty partners rather than any general rule of law. Even a large number of treaties of commerce or of investment guaranty or agreements for the settlement of international claims may either affirm or negate the existence of a rule of international law, depending on whether they are considered to be declaratory of a general norm of international law or derogations from a body of law which recognizes no obligation of full, adequate, or just compensation. Of general international conventions "establishing rules expressly recognized by the contesting states" there is effectively none binding on a substantial number of developing and developed states.

The practice of states with respect to compensation for nationalized property is so diverse that one cannot speak of any "international custom, as evidence of a general practice accepted as law," as the Statute refers to customary international law.

Study of the nationalization and valuation of property has quite properly led to an examination of the rules applied in national legal systems, whether to the nationalization of the property of aliens or the taking of property of nationals. Several essays in

Volume I deal with the valuation of nationalized property under foreign legal systems, and the same theme is taken up in Professor Furnish's study of petroleum expropriations in Bolivia and Peru and by Professor Goldman and Mr. Paxman in their survey of the municipal law of property valuation in Argentina, Chile, and Mexico. But it is difficult to derive from such a study of national legal systems any "general principles of law recognized by civilized nations" which have sufficient content to guide the decision of specific cases. The standards of real property valuation employed in Argentina, Chile, and Mexico are shown to be in a number of material respects quite different from those employed in common law countries, for example. The emphasis on the value of property as established for the assessment of taxes is a striking feature of this study of Latin American practice.

That leaves the subsidiary means for the determination of rules of law, "judicial decisions" and the "teachings of the most highly qualified publicists." What judicial decisions there are fail to carry weight with many states. Their age, the difficulty of determining the precise extent of their holdings, the difference between the social and economic conditions of the past and those of today, changes in the nature of foreign investment, and the international relations of the past which gave rise to the decisions make them suspect in the eyes of many states turning to nationalization of foreign property as a means of dealing with their economic problems. The *Lena Goldfields Arbitration,* the *Delagoa Bay Case,* and nineteenth- and early twentieth-century arbitrations between the United States and nations of Latin America command allegiance in the United States and other developed countries but they signify little in other quarters of the world. Decisions of the International Court in The Hague bearing on nationalization are few and fail to confront the main issues of standard and of valuation. The disposition by the International Court of Justice of the *Barcelona Traction Company Case* destroyed any hope that might have existed that the International Court of Justice would pronounce itself on the questions of valuation discussed by Dr. White in her study in Volume I of this work.

A number of "eminent publicists," amongst whom must be numbered the editor of this volume, have attempted to give expression to rules of international law on the nationalization of property, but there has certainly been no uniformity of views amongst these "eminent publicists" from different quarters of the world and from different legal systems.

In the absence of any firm evidence of international law, what purpose can be served by a study such as this one, which looks to the theory of valuation, the practice of national claims commissions, individual settlements, and the state of the law in various countries? While their contents may not be direct contributions to international law, they do represent a stock of solutions, a way of looking at things, an analysis of the issues, and a fruitful source of analogy and example. The battle over nationalization and valuation may be partly won if the contending parties can be persuaded to conduct their dispute with these weapons. Concepts drawn from other spheres can become part of the vocabulary of debate. Accumulated instances establish standards of relevance. They impart criteria of fundamental fairness from other forums and other legal systems. They establish the ground on which the game is played and some of the rules and "plays" of the game. Metaphor comes naturally, as one gropes for a way of describing sources and evidence of international law that are not in themselves authoritative guides to decision but supply accumulated wisdom and juristic concepts for those who must make decisions or arrive at compromises.

One cannot read these two volumes without acquiring a more sophisticated way of viewing problems of valuation. And certainly if adversaries were to inform themselves from these books, they would have a deeper understanding of the issues and, one might hope, the means of understanding each other and of finding common ground.

One can no longer speak of valuation as a field in which "ignorant armies clash by night." The clashes may continue, but the armies will no longer be ignorant ones.

R. R. BAXTER

Cambridge, Massachusetts
November 1972

Preface

When *The Valuation of Nationalized Property in International Law*[1] appeared some months ago, one reviewer noted that it was "th[e] first serious effort to explore in detail the process and standards of valuation."[2] Another generously suggested that "[i]f this book enjoys the reception it merits, the editor should be encouraged to assay one or more sequels."[3] The present volume, to be followed by a third and final one including contributions by Communist and Third World writers plus several essays of an overview nature, is being published in response to this encouragement.

Like its predecessor, "[t]his collection of seven essays is not the systematic analysis of this important problem that is so urgently needed. Rather, it is a loosely structured attempt to identify problems and recommended solutions in a number of areas where the contributors have some degree of expertise."[4] The interdisciplinary approach taken in the first volume, moreover, is reflected in the present one, which includes chapters by a leading accountant and an eminent economist. So, too, is the comparative approach, with the final chapter once again comparing various municipal law valuation standards—this time those of Argentina, Chile, and Mexico—both with each other and with the norms of international law.[5]

Concern with the process and standards of valuation, of course, is most relevant when the principle of compensation is not disputed. When countries reject this principle for ideological reasons,

---

[1] The Valuation of Nationalized Property in International Law (R. Lillich ed. & contrib. 1972).

[2] Theberge, Book Review, 6 Int'l Lawyer 667, 668 (1972).

[3] Laylin, Book Review, 12 Va. J. Int'l L. 282 (1972).

[4] *Preface* to The Valuation of Nationalized Property in International Law, *supra* note 1, at xii.

[5] This chapter is responsive to the suggestion by one reviewer of the first volume that "[i]f the editor brings out a sequel, it is to be hoped it will provide student and practitioner alike with information as to the practice in countries not covered in this book. . . ." Laylin, *supra* note 3, at 284. *Cf.* Expropriation in the Americas: A Comparative Law Study (A. Lowenfeld ed. 1971)).

as the Soviet Union did after the Russian Revolution,[6] or when they engage in what Evelyn Waugh once called "robbery under law,"[7] as may be happening in the case of Chile, the question of valuation is obviously of lesser, albeit still significant, importance. The focus upon valuation, however, in no way represents an attempt "to avoid the more complex, emotional and troublesome issues of compensation and nationalization."[8] Rather, it is intentionally designed to shed some light upon the one area where international lawyers, in the opinion of this writer, can make a contribution to the development of some reasonable and workable standards. Recent negotiations between the international oil companies and the OPEC states over the amount of compensation the latter should pay to acquire 25 percent participation interests in the companies' local operations underscore the practical as well as jurisprudential importance of studies taking the approach reflected in these volumes.[9]

This writer wishes to express his appreciation to the other contributors to the volume who have produced four original and two revised essays of considerable merit. He also wishes to acknowledge the kind permission of the *Kentucky Law Journal* and the *International Lawyer* to draw upon material published in and copyrighted by them as the basis for the essays comprising Chapters IV and VI and to record his thanks to the Kennecott Copper Corporation for permission to publish a portion of its so-called "White Paper"[10] as Chapter V. Finally, once again the Publications Committee of the University of Virginia School of Law deserves recognition for the encouragement and support that has made this venture possible.

RICHARD B. LILLICH

Charlottesville, Virginia
September 1972

[6] *See generally* K. GRZYBOWSKI, SOVIET PUBLIC INTERNATIONAL LAW 82–88 (1970).

[7] E. WAUGH, ROBBERY UNDER LAW: THE MEXICAN OBJECT LESSON (1939).

[8] Theberge, *supra* note 2, at 667.

[9] *See* THE ECONOMIST, Sept. 16, 1972, at 91, col. 1. "It now seems that the compensation will be based on little more than the net book value of the assets involved, with slight allowance made for the future potential of the international companies' rights." *Id.*

[10] KENNECOTT COPPER CORPORATION, EXPROPRIATION OF EL TENIENTE (1971).

Contents

The General Perspective

CHAPTER I

The Compensation Rule:
An Imaginary Debate

Thomas F. Bergin

EDITORS of casebooks on American property law are fond of inserting early in their books Bentham's famous dictum: "Property and law are born together, and die together. Before laws were made there was no property; take away laws, and property ceases." The dictum is useful, for it alerts students to the fact that the cases they will be studying will not be merely examples of judicial application of given rules to found facts but will often be examples of how courts manufacture "property" by exercise of the judicial will. Armed by this pre-Realist hint that "property," in the lawyer's sense, does not exactly come to us trailing clouds of glory, students are more likely, or so the editors hope, to be able to accept the intellectual task of challenging and criticizing the judge-made rules they will be studying. If property is the result of law, and law is the result of human choice, then property is the result of human choice. The logic is inexorable, and so is the classroom inquiry that follows upon it; for it is plainly the case that property law courses in most law schools in the United States today are aimed less at imparting the rules than at testing their social usefulness in various conflict settings. Although it is possible that some property law teachers have convinced themselves that dysfunctional judge-made rules cannot be part of law at all, most of them, one imagines, simply accept the premise that sound rules will likely command more willing assent than unsound ones.

All of which is by way of warning that this chapter will not attempt to answer the question whether there is, or is not, a rule of international law which commands nations to pay compensation to foreign nationals whose property they take. In the style and mode of the contemporary property law course, this chapter will be directed to the question whether reasons for having a compensation rule can be found with sufficient generality to command assent even by nations that do not compensate their own nationals on the occasion of a taking. Although the writer will offer his own answer to that question, he asks the reader to regard his answer as tentative only—perhaps more the product of fatigue than of wisdom.

It is, of course, near to preposterous to expect lawyer-readers of this chapter to suspend for a time their certain knowledge that an international compensation rule does, or does not, exist, or even to acknowledge perplexity at the certain fact that others are certain they are wrong. It is even closer to preposterous to ask those lawyer-readers to forget for a time that rules of law that might have, when first proposed, been judged by an overwhelming majority of reflective and moral men as inefficient or immoral, can, by official promulgation, become efficient and moral by reason of the clustering of expectations about them; for rules that develop, by application only, their own excuse for being are as much the stuff of lawyers' law as rules that commanded rational and moral assent from the moment of their conception. Yet the effort must be asked, for it is precisely a *tabula rasa* world into which readers of this chapter are invited to step.

I. SETTING FOR AN IMAGINARY DEBATE

Our unreal setting is as follows: Although nation-states have come into being and have adopted their own municipal laws regulating the affairs of their own nationals, trade and travel among the nations have not yet started. By reason, however, of the recent invention of ocean-going vessels, it has become apparent that trade and travel among the nations may now proceed. It also has become sadly apparent that international aggression has become a distinct possibility. Fortunately, the leaders of the nations are all peaceful men, and they have already agreed unanimously that no nation may seek to improve its well-being by using force against any other nation.

Those leaders are now meeting in what they have termed a constitutive assembly of nations to establish international rules of trade and investment. Although the leaders regard it as likely that some of the nations are rich in natural resources and others are poor, they do not know which are the rich ones and which the poor. As a matter of fact, they have agreed not to try to find out which are rich and which are poor lest that knowledge improperly cant their judgment about the proposed rules they will be considering. Choosing in the dark, they have agreed, will force them to give fair consideration to the least favored nations, for their own nations may prove to be among that group. They also have agreed that no proposed rule will be deemed adopted except upon a unanimous vote. Although the nations, up to this point, have existed wholly independently of one another, they have all developed fairly sophisticated systems of thought about the nature and meaning of "property." We also may conceive of some of them as having independently achieved a fairly advanced level of economic productivity. The leaders assembled are all of the view that cooperation in the production of useful goods will be of benefit to all the nations, for they perceive that each of the nations will likely enjoy some kind of comparative advantage over the others in productive techniques, natural resources, availability of labor, or what have you. The chief idea of the meeting is to find ways in which those comparative advantages can be used for the betterment of all the nations.

With just a little bit of luck, we find this remarkable group of world leaders just beginning to pry open the question whether there ought to be an international compensation rule. What is rapidly becoming apparent, as speaker after speaker explains his own nation's property law, is that there is little congruence in the theories and philosophies sustaining those laws. A rough classification of the nations suggests that there are four main groups. One group of nations, which we may call the Inherent Rights Group, is committed to the principle that exclusive private enjoyment of economic goods has been ordained by God. A national of one of these nations is viewed as simply endowed by his Creator with the right to acquire things in order to achieve his own humanity. Although there are legal restraints on the ways in which ownership can be acquired, once ownership is lawfully acquired owners are free to use goods as they wish. This freedom is thought necessary, for man is put on earth to be tested by God. By owning things, he is free to sin or to do charity. Owners are not answerable to the state; they are answerable only to God. A characteristic of the property laws of these nations is that they label "unjust" the taking by government of private property without payment of compensation. The purpose of the compensation is to restore the loser to the state of personal self-realization he had achieved before the taking.

A second group of nations, which we may call the Custodial Theory Group, gives legal protection to private claims to economic goods, but they justify this protection on social welfare grounds. Persons so protected are viewed as social custodians of the nation's wealth, and they are expected to make use choices that will promote the common good. Oddly enough, these nations do not prescribe in any significant detail the range of use choices that the custodians may make. Nor, apparently, do they count upon the natural benignity of the custodians to move resources to socially desired uses. Quite to the contrary, they seem to assume that the custodians will be selfish men—or, to use the softer term common in these nations, "utility-maximizers." The intellectual theory which the leaders of these nations offer to resolve this seeming paradox of selfishness harnessed in service of society is essentially the following: Assuming that the custodians have a healthy share of human avarice, they will naturally put goods in their custody to those uses which promise them the highest possible personal gain. Since money votes in the marketplace reflect more sensitively than political votes the real preferences of the people, and since allocation by the market is less costly than political allocation, it makes much sense to allow the custodians to sell the goods in their custody to persons who vote the most money to get them. If the custodians are allowed to keep the money paid for the goods, those goods will be led, as if by an invisible hand, to achieve the best good for all. The nice thing about the system, as the leaders explain, is that nobody is ever made worse off by its operation. Since trade in goods is always voluntary, it is plain that aggregate welfare is always moving upwards; for why else would people willingly trade except to move to preferred positions?

It is interesting to note that nations in the Custodial Theory Group also label "unjust'" governmental takings of property without payment of compensation; but it is plain that the function of their compensation rules is different from the function assigned to compensation rules by nations in the Inherent Rights Group. Nations in the Custodial Theory Group require compensation for two related purposes: to restrain government from putting goods to low-value uses and to assure the custodians that they need not, out of fear of government action, make hasty and inefficient allocations. These twin purposes are accomplished by requiring government to pay "full and fair market value" to persons whose property it takes. In these nations, the "injustice" of an uncompensated taking lies in its potential misallocative effect.

A third group of nations, which we may term the Soft Socialist Group, seems committed to the view that private ownership of basic natural resources and of so-called "key industries" that use those resources for the production of essential goods and services leads not only to an undemocratic concentration of political and economic power in the hands of the private owners but also to an inadequate provision of those goods and services and an inequitable distribution of the national income. During the past fifty or so years, these nations have been "nationalizing" ownership of these basic resources and key industries, converting them from private to public ownership. In theory, resources and industries that have been nationalized are simply directed by the democratic political process, but in actual practice management responsibility lies chiefly with professional planners who are directed to act in the public interest.

Although the political philosophies of nations in the Soft Socialist Group appear to be marked by a strong strain of egalitarianism, there is broad recognition of the principle that fair compensation must be paid to persons whose goods are taken for public use. One gathers that the compensation is not required to restrain governmental takings, but rather to protect expectations of owners. Such expectations are viewed as components of the national aggregate well-being, and the purpose of compensation is to prevent political majorities from exacting disproportionate sacrifice from any citizen.

The fourth group, which we may label the Hard Socialist Group, shares the common faith that man is part of, and caught up within, an organic historical process of conflict between persons who create value by their labor and persons who, by ownership of scarce resources, expropriate or usurp part of that value without contributing to it. These would-be (or used-to-be, in the case of some of the nations in this group) expropriators or usurpers, termed "capitalists," are not violators of God's commands, for a personal god is not recognized in these nations. Their sinfulness is wholly secular; it lies in their willful resistance to the inevitable reassertion by those persons who labor of their full rights to the value they create. Since the capitalists never compensate persons whose property-in-labor they steal, there is no reason why they should be compensated when the workers "take back" from the capitalists the resources and capital goods that never rightfully belonged to the capitalists anyway. Once those resources and capital goods are taken back, these nations believe, there will inevitably emerge a social system marked by cooperative egalitarianism. Men will willingly labor together for the benefit of all, and the national productive wealth will be distributed equitably according to need.

Notwithstanding the obvious incongruence of the philosophies of property adhered to within the nations now in conclave, there is uniform agreement among them that mutual cooperation in the production of useful goods can be of benefit to all of them. A motion having now been made and duly seconded that all nations be bound to compensate foreign nationals whose property they take, discussion of the motion is about to proceed.

II. THE IMAGINARY DEBATE

The first speaker to be recognized is a leader of a nation in the Hard Socialist Group. "As I understand the motion," he begins, "it contemplates the possibility of private citizens of one nation acquiring property in the natural resources and capital goods of another nation. Were I to vote for the motion, I should regard myself as not merely violating an article of man-made political faith, but an objective law of social process which governs us all. In my own nation we have been able, by standing apart from that process in order to observe it scientifically, to see the direction in which it moves man. Man lives in a world of scarcity and natural equality. The laws of his nature ordain that he struggle to survive. This struggle leads him to deny to any man the right to convert scarce goods to his personal ends, for such conversion entails denial to others of the right to survive. I view the motion, as would the workers in my country, as essentially reactionary, for it plainly contemplates return to a system in which those who labor are made the slaves of those who do not."

The second speaker to be recognized is a leader of a nation in the Inherent Rights Group. "The motion does contemplate," he begins, "precisely what the previous speaker suggested: full private ownership by citizens of one nation of productive resources located within the physical boundaries of another nation. In my nation, as I indicated earlier when I explained our property law, such full ownership is judged to be necessary for the achievement of self. It is our profound faith that man is invested with a spiritual component which moves him to fashion out of the physical stuff about him a personal statement of his being. To deny him the right to acquire and use economic goods as his conscience dictates is to deny him the chance to demonstrate his worthiness before God. To be sure, we acknowledge that man's law must fix the boundaries of appropriative action by individuals; but we cannot concede to any collectivity the moral right to bar private acquisition of wealth or to seize acquired wealth for something called the common good without payment of full compensation. I support the motion because I devoutly believe that it expresses the Universal Will."

The third speaker to speak to the motion is a leader from the Custodial Theory Group. "The two previous speakers," he commences, "have made the common error of treating the motion as a declaration of philosophy or faith. Properly understood, the motion is nothing of the sort; it is merely a pledge to engage in a certain kind of conduct, or negatively, to refrain from a certain kind of conduct. The first speaker, as I understood him, opposed the motion because it would, as he viewed it, put him on record as supporting private entitlement to productive resources. Yet it is plain that the motion, if adopted, would require no nation to allow foreign nationals to acquire resources within its boundaries. Any nation that chose to shut its doors to resource-seeking foreign nationals—call them capitalists or saints, as you will—would be free to do so. I should also suppose, though the motion is not clear on the point, that nations would be able to 'contract out' of the compensation rule by conditioning an investor's entry upon his willing and explicit acceptance of the risk of not being compensated should a taking occur. As I read the motion, it says simply this: *If* a nation *chooses* to allow a foreign national to acquire resources within its boundaries, and *if* that nation does not secure from that investor an explicit expression of his willingness to run the risk of not being compensated should those resources be taken from him, then it must compensate him if it does take those resources.

"I support the motion, myself," the third speaker continues, "precisely because it does contemplate voluntariness. No nation will allow a foreign national to acquire resources within its boundaries unless it is satisfied that it will be getting more than it gives up. That 'more' may be in the form of technical skill, capital equipment, title to specific resources in the investor's nation, or money claims backed up by the productive capacity of the investor's nation. By the same token, no investor will seek to acquire resources in another nation unless he is satisfied that acquiring them will make him better off. There will, of course, be risks on both sides, for the future cannot be known; but if risk taking is voluntary, it implies that the risk takers regard themselves as moving to preferred positions. One final point, and I am done. It is plain to me that we are not here to dissolve our separate nations into a single 'Nation of the Earth' or even to frame an internation utility principle which would entail acceptance of the idea that one nation may involuntarily be made worse off if the change produces a *net gain* in aggregate *world* welfare. It ought to be noted, therefore, that the voluntary trading in resources of the sort contemplated by the motion produces *absolute* gains in the aggregate welfare of both capital-import and capital-export nations. Aggregate world welfare moves upwards with no sacrifice of the well-being of any nation."

The fourth speaker to address the assembly on the motion is a leader from the Soft Socialist Group. "The speaker who has just preceded me," he begins, "laments any characterization of the motion as a declaration of philosophy or faith. He then proceeds to launch into what can only be termed a sermon in support of the free market. We have had a bit of experience with the free market in my country, and our faith in its ability to carry mankind to a Golden Realm on Earth is something less than profound. The free market produces absolute gains in aggregate welfare only if the level of welfare of the trading parties *before trade* is taken as given. Take the case of the robber who says to his proposed victim: 'Your money or your life.' It is, of course, *given* that the proposed victim's *immediate* state of well-being—his well-being while the robbery proceeds—is very low; for the robber quite literally owns his life at least in the sense of having power to dispose of it. Ah, but the robber has offered a chance to engage in voluntary trade. If the proposed victim *chooses,* he can hand over his money in exchange for the pleasure of continuing to breathe and see sunset's glow. If he accepts the bargain—as he likely will, for it is surely the bargain of his life—we shall certainly have to say that both parties have moved to preferred positions. Aggregate welfare will have moved up absolutely because both parties will regard themselves as better off than they were just before the offer was accepted.

"Now, it will be objected," the fourth speaker continues, "that the example I have given is not truly one of voluntary trade because the victim had no 'real' choice. Moreover, the change in aggregate well-being in my example was not a change from one *law-recognized* level to a higher *law-recognized* level. True enough, but is it not in fact the case that in societies that rely upon the free market to increase aggregate well-being the law itself often recognizes states of well-being that shock the civilized conscience? Change the robbery victim in my example to a man who is poor because he has no skill to sell in the marketplace and change the robber to a man who owns all the milk-producing cows. The power of the cow owner over the poor man is, in my mind, indistinguishable from the power of the robber over his victim; yet when the poor man hands over his last ten ducats to buy milk for his starving child—to buy his child's life, so to speak—the free-market priests rush to tell us that aggregate welfare has moved up absolutely.

"I recognize," the fourth speaker continues, "that I am using up more than my fair share of time; but please allow me to relate my parables to the motion before us. Implicit in that motion, as I understand it, is the notion that a nation will never have the right wholly to repudiate a foreign national's title to resources within its boundaries. If it wishes to regain ownership of such resources, it will have to buy the investor off by paying enough to make him whole. But might it not be the case that the original bargain offered by the investor was as brutally unfair as the bargains offered by the robber and milk monopolist in my examples? Might it not also be the case that the leaders of the government that struck the bargain with the investor were corrupt and that they used their power to deny the citizens their own birthright by selling the national assets for personal gain? Until I am satisfied that the bargaining powers of nations and of those who would invest in them are reasonably equal and until I am satisfied that the governments of all the nations are as free of corruption and as reflective of the common will as the government of my own nation, I cannot vote for a motion which extends the protection of law to all bargains."

"Mr. Chairman!" It is the third speaker who is angrily addressing the chair. "I rise on a point of personal privilege." On being recognized, the third speaker proceeds: "The gentleman who has just addressed us has plainly violated the rules of civilized debate by characterizing me and others who share my views as 'free-market priests' and by crudely suggesting that some of the leaders here may be corrupt. More importantly, he has fouled our debate by indulging in a kind of conundrum making which, he imagines, will have us gasping at his intellect. I, for one, gasp less at his intellect than at his ability to contrive nonsense out of the same words that other men use to create useful ideas.

"The intellectual emptiness of the last speaker's remarks," the third speaker continues, "can be easily demonstrated. He refuses to vote for the motion, because it may give protection to bargains that are later found to have been unfair or corruptly made. To him, it is fundamentally wrong that law should be regarded as so fixing entitlements to well-being as to make meaningful the statement that a poor man's well-being moves up when he engages in voluntary trade. But I should have thought it untrivially true that the fixing of entitlements to well-being and of procedures through which such entitlements may change is the only function that law performs. Consider, for example, the legal concept of contract. Would it be meaningful in any way to talk of contracts between men if there were not given by law some beginning set of entitlements? When *A* contracts to buy a cow from *B*, he need not concede that *B* owns the cow; but he must concede that he, *A*, does *not* own it. It is, of course, law that compels that concession from him. Similarly, it is law that fixes entitlement to life itself, thereby making criminal various life-taking acts. Killing of human beings can precede and follow law; but murder can only follow law. I remind the previous speaker that the prelaw state of nature in which he would like to leave the nations of the world—pending, of course, his being 'satisfied' that law will not protect unfair baragins—is precisely that state in which the weak are truly at the mercy of the strong. I remind him also that it is a little bit late to be suggesting that we ought not to be fixing the entitlements of the nations here assembled; for before this conference met, the nations of the world unanimously agreed that no nation may seek to improve its well-being by using force against any other nation. That was, gentlemen, a fixing of entitlements by law. Since those entitlements cannot be changed by force, it is plain they can only be changed by voluntary trade."

The first speaker who addressed the assembly on the motion is again being recognized by the chair. "Mr. Chairman and comrades," he begins, "in my country we have a saying: The wind whistles in the forest because it is afraid. The comments of the last two speakers have sounded to me much like the wind whistling in the forest, which prompts me to wonder of what they are afraid? My suspicion—it is only that—is that they are afraid of the people. The fourth speaker who addressed us today—the one who refused to vote for the motion until he was satisfied it did not extend the protection of law to unfair or corrupt bargains—sounds to me much like the capitalist who, sensing that the workers are about to take to the streets, quickly drapes himself out as one of them in order to move among them offering soft assurances that the government is truly on their side. If only he can persuade them that it is the big monopolists who oppress them, and not the ordinary bourgeoisie, they may, he hopes, put their trust in what he will call 'the democratic process.' He will, of course, talk much about the 'unfairness of the income distribution' and the 'heartlessness of the free market,' but he will never suggest that private property itself is the foundry in which their chains are cast, for his job is to hold back the mob. But easier it would be to hold back the ocean tides, for the workers will not be deceived.

"Nor will the workers be long cajoled," the first speaker continues, "by the tendentious casuistry that marked the third speaker's peroration on the thaumaturgic qualities of the free market. To see how the free market works, they have merely to look at the swollen bellies of their children. The third speaker would have us believe that our previous commitment to refrain from the use of force in the pursuit of national well-being was, if only we would recognize it, the establishment of an international law of property. Since force cannot be used to change the entitlements fixed by that law, the only mechanism of change left to us is contract. But he neglects to inform us when it may properly be said that contract has effected a change in entitlements. Is it to be the case that a change of entitlements will be deemed to have been effected when the contract bargainers agree that change has occurred? But suppose that one of the bargainers did not own the assets he sold. Suppose he stole them from the workers. Is it to be the case that the workers cannot reassert their lawful title? If that is to be the case, then our resolution against the use of force becomes a resolution never to change our own internal rules of entitlement once a foreign national has relied upon their semblance as law. I do not read our resolution against force that way. I read it simply as an undertaking of the nations not to launch armed attacks upon one another. To read it as freezing domestic rules of entitlement is not merely to alter its plain meaning; it is to give it no meaning at all; for how, other than by force, could the workers of any nation be barred from throwing thieves out of power? It is, I suggest, an inverted alchemy which converts a resolution against force into a veiled threat to use force.

"Our problem here," the first speaker continues, "comes down to this. We perceive that opportunities for fruitful cooperation in the production of useful goods likely exist, and we agree that contract is the only mechanism through which that cooperation can be achieved. But we cannot agree on the principles by which it is to be determined whether a contract party had, or had not, the lawful authority to commit his nation's resources to the bargain he struck. Some of you may regard my view that the workers are the true owners of all productive resources as distasteful or even contrary to the will of your god; but you must recognize that I view your positions as equally detestable.

"The question to which we must direct ourselves," the first speaker continues, "is whether we can break out of our dilemma and at the same time preserve intact our national philosophies of property and our national rights to change our internal rules of entitlement. At this stage in our proceedings, I am inclined to think that the best way to escape our dilemma is simply to vote down the motion that put us in it. Let me invite you to consider what would happen if the motion were voted down. Would it be the case that meaningful investment bargains could never be struck? I should suppose it would not. The fact that international law did not stamp investment bargains as beyond repudiation would simply be a factor to be taken account of in the bargaining process. Prospective investors in the resources of other nations would, out of prudence, concern themselves with the rules of entitlement existing in those nations and also with the likelihood or unlikelihood of changes in those rules. In cases where the likelihood of change seemed high, the investors would, presumably, either refrain from investing or adjust their bids to reflect the risks. Similarly, nations seeking to gain by allowing foreign nationals to acquire resources within their boundaries would undoubtedly concern themselves with the rules of entitlement obtaining in the prospective investors' nations; for it is plain that investors too commit their nations' resources to their bargains. Now, I am certain it will be argued that if we do not adopt the motion, the costs of international investment trade will be much increased by reason of the additional negotiation that will be necessary for investors and nations to obtain *by bargain* what the motion gives them *by law.* Yet, is it not clearly the case that since the motion does not call for the use of force to compel nations to pay compensation to foreign nationals, the political risk factors to which I have alluded will necessarily be in the bargaining mix even if the motion passes? We must keep in mind, comrades, that there may be those among us today who do not have the lawful authority even to bind their nations to the constitutive rules we imagine we are establishing."

The Chairman is now addressing the assembly. "Gentleman, I am prepared to accept a call for the question, but I do not want to close off discussion before all views have been ventilated. I see that the second speaker who addressed us on the motion wishes to be recognized. I will recognize the gentleman, but perhaps we can agree that discussion will close with this gentleman's remarks. Proceed, sir."

"It is plain to me," the second speaker begins, "that the gentleman who has just addressed us has brought the only real issue before us into sharp focus. That issue, very simply, is whether any nation, after having allowed a foreign national to acquire resources within its boundaries, may so change its internal rules of entitlement as to repudiate the foreign national's title. Since such repudiation would, by hypothesis, be based upon the theory that the transfer of title to the foreign national was, *ab initio,* unlawful and, hence, a legal nullity, compensation would, presumably, not be required. It will surprise you, I imagine, when I tell you that I believe the motion before us can, in fact, be invested with substantive meaning even though it is interpreted as authorizing nations to repudiate, as unlawful *ab initio,* transfers of title to foreign nationals; but before I explain to you how I reconcile that interpretation with my profound conviction that private property is ordained by God, please allow me to direct a few words to the previous speaker's suggestion that adoption of the motion will not reduce bargaining costs in international investment trade.

"That suggestion," the second speaker continues, "reveals a remarkable lack of insight about the nature of the law we create if we adopt the motion. Since the motion does not contemplate the use of force to compel nations to compensate foreign nationals, it cannot, the previous speaker argues, reduce bargaining costs between nations and investors; for they will have to take into account political risk factors, including, of course, possible *ex post facto* changes in internal rules of entitlement. But suppose for a moment that the motion were adopted unanimously and that we all agreed that it was intended to *bar* such *ex post facto* changes. Would prospective bargainers be unable to count on it to protect them from such changes? I am convinced that they would be able to count on it, for any nation that violated the rule would immediately brand itself as unworthy of the confidence of the community of nations. Once a nation so stained itself, no amount of talk about the 'unlawfulness' of the consent which it earlier gave to the rule would persuade the other nations that it was now worthy of their trust. My point, gentlemen, is that the rules we make here may meaningfully be called 'law' even though they are not backed by force. No law is stronger than the consent that sustains it, and that applies, I am sure, even to our own municipal laws.

"Now, let me return," the second speaker continues, "to the substantive issue before us. I said a moment ago that I believe the motion before us can be invested with meaning even if it is interpreted as allowing nations to repudiate, as unlawful *ab initio,* transfers of title to foreign nationals. How might that be accomplished? By simply interpreting the motion as barring nations from *unjustly enriching themselves by changing their internal rules of entitlement.* So interpreted, the motion concedes the right of nations to repudiate transfers of title to foreign nationals. It also technically concedes the right of nations to refuse to pay compensation *for the recovery of title* which, by hypothesis, was never in the foreign nationals in the first place. But what the motion does not concede is that nations may retain, without payment, the benefits of bargains that they later brand unlawful.

"What I am proposing, gentlemen," the second speaker continues, "is the injection into our motion of a *substantive principle of fairness.* Implicit in my proposed interpretation of the motion is the notion that investment bargains can, in fact, be appraised by reasonable and fair-minded men as deserving of the protection of law or not deserving of it. The adjudicative process that would follow upon the repudiation by a nation of a foreign national's title would not be directed at determining whether the repudiation was lawful, for that would be conceded, but rather whether the repudiating nation had, by using its *lawful power* to change its rules of entitlement, gained an unjust advantage. In order to resolve that issue, the adjudicators would, in a sense, put the parties to the bargain back in the bargaining phase. The question to be answered would be this: What would a *fair and reasonable* investor have asked to be paid for the benefits that this investor has actually bestowed upon this nation, and what would a *fair and reasonable* nation have reasonably been willing to pay for the benefits that this nation has actually received? As you can see, it is entirely possible that an investor would be made whole as a result of the adjudication. It is even possible, though substantially less likely, that the adjudicators would find that the original bargain had been unfair to the investor, and that he was entitled to more compensation than he had actually won through negotiation. The adjudicative procedure that I have in mind is rather in the nature of a proceeding to reform a contract. Compensation awarded to foreign nationals would not be for 'property' taken from them, but rather for the fair and reasonable value of benefits they had conferred.

"I can see that I have already exhausted your patience," the second speaker continues, "but please allow me to make two final points about the interpretation I have proposed. The first point is this: I am much aware that my interpretation does not afford full protection to the investor who, by reason of the repudiation of his title, is denied the opportunity to confer *additional* benefits. Since he will be paid only for benefits conferred *before repudiation,* he may not enjoy the full change in his revenue position that he expected when he entered his bargain. Although one might be tempted to cure this deficiency by stating that fair and reasonable bargains must be given full legal effect—*i.e.,* that repudiations of title will be regarded, where bargains were fair and reasonable, as contract breaches entitling investors to full recovery of lost profit—that would, in my opinion, put us back in the dilemma from which we were seeking to escape. If nations will not permit their repudiations of titles to be second-guessed by international adjudicative tribunals, they will surely not allow such tribunals to second-guess their repudiations of the bargains on which those titles are founded. To escape our dilemma, we must, I believe, concede that both titles and the bargains on which they are founded may be repudiated. To do that, however, is not to convert the motion into an engraved invitation to nations to repudiate either titles or bargains; for nations that so treat it will undoubtedly reduce their opportunities for future profitable trade with others. In a word, repudiation will be a self-punishing act.

"My final point," the second speaker goes on, "is this: My proposed interpretation of the motion offers no protection to the investor in cases where the benefits he actually conferred were diverted by corrupt persons to their own pockets. This results from the fact that my interpretation contemplates his being paid the fair value of benefits conferred upon the *nation* in which he invests—not its corrupt citizens. Here again, we might be tempted to tinker with words to cure the deficiency—for example, by saying that benefits received by corrupt citizens of any nation must be counted as increasing that nation's aggregate well-being. But I would urge that we not do so, lest we tinker the motion into unacceptability. By leaving the deficiency uncured by law, we do not, of course, leave investors without any protection; for most nations will hesitate to repudiate even corruptly made bargains for fear of losing repute among the trading nations. Moreover, it will likely often be the case that repudiating nations will be able to recover from their corrupt citizens some or all of the benefits that they converted. Under my interpretation of the motion, nations will be obliged to make that effort. Yet, it must be conceded that the risk of loss is a real one. I fear, gentlemen, that it is a risk which the nature of our circumstances makes inevitable."

III. EPILOGUE

The reader of this chapter has correctly inferred that the interpretation of the motion offered by the final speaker is the one which the author finds most appealing, but it has not been the author's intent to offer a final resolution of the compensation issue. That issue will long remain an open one, for it goes centrally to one of the most perplexing problems of international law: that of reconciling the right, if it is that, of nations to change their municipal rules with the right, if it is that, of other nations and their nationals to rely upon the continuance of those municipal rules. If there is a point to be made by this chapter, it is not that the final speaker's interpretation of the motion was right; it is simply that debate on the compensation question cannot fruitfully proceed if nations persist upon believing that their own philosophies of "property" uniquely capture the final wisdom of mankind.

CHAPTER II

An Economic Analysis of Aspects of International Expropriation of Property

Norman N. Mintz

SINCE the end of the Second World War there have been hundreds of cases of expropriation by foreign nations of property owned by nationals of other countries. In many of these cases of expropriation, the taking government has compensated, to a greater or lesser extent, the former owners of the property or their governments; in other cases no compensation has been paid.

The requirement that compensation be paid by taking governments is well established in international law.[1] In some cases the governments of the former owners of taken property actually have gone so far as to make monetary concessions to taking governments so as to induce the payment of compensation and maintain the legal fiction that such compensation had been paid, *i.e.*, to reenforce the international legal precedents requiring compensation.[2]

Because knowledge of expropriation, that is, of international property rights, is a natural part of the equipment of international lawyers, the legal literature in the area is vast. Traditional legal doctrine holds that compensation paid for taken property should be prompt, adequate, and effective.[3] Forays into economics by legal scholars have tended to be only for the purpose of defining these terms, particularly the term "adequate," and so there is also a literature concerned with estimating the value of taken property, including debate as to the merits of alternative methods of evaluation.[4]

The author is grateful to the Columbia University Council for Research in the Social Sciences for financial support.

[1] On December 14, 1962, by a vote of 87 to 2 with 12 abstentions, the United Nations General Assembly voted that persons deprived of their property "shall be paid appropriate compensation . . . in accordance with international law." *See* R. Lillich, The Protection of Foreign Investment 83 (1965).

[2] In Mintz, *Economic Observations on Lump Sum Settlements Agreements*, 43 Ind. L.J. 885 (1968), it was shown that the United States' economic concessions to Rumania, Bulgaria, and Poland followed closely upon and largely financed those countries' compensation agreements with the United States.

[3] But legal scholars are widening their horizons. *See* Dawson & Weston, *"Prompt, Adequate and Effective": A Universal Standard of Compensation?*, 30 Fordham L. Rev. 727 (1962).

[4] *See, e.g.*, Panel Discussion, *The Taking of Property: Evaluation of Damages*, 62 Am. Soc'y Int'l Proceedings 35 (1968). *See also* The Valuation of Nationalized Property in International Law (R. Lillich ed. & contrib. 1972).

Although there are a few efforts by economists *qua* economists to examine expropriation,[5] the balance of effort is weighted heavily in favor of legal scholars. This chapter is an effort to redress that balance slightly.

One of the contentions of this chapter is that the frame of reference in which one views expropriation tends to color one's analysis of the effects of expropriation. Section I suggests an approach which, though not unusual in economic analysis, has not been applied consistently to the examination of international expropriation. Section II attempts to integrate expropriation into the general theory of international trade, while Section III expands the analysis slightly to take account of some aspects of income distribution. Section IV discusses certain effects of expropriation external to the economic system as such. Section V discusses, perhaps too briefly and superficially, some of the policy implications of the analysis that has preceded it.

I. STOCKS *VERSUS* FLOWS IN THE ANALYSIS OF EXPROPRIATION

Perhaps the only aspect of expropriation on which virtually all writers and official bodies agree is that taken property has some value;[6] though that value may not be unambiguously ascertainable it is assumed to be positive. This view, which finds its philosophical bases in the concept of property rights, gives analytical primacy to the stock of assets, which, as a result of expropriation, change ownership. Such an analytical frame of reference may be justified in a variety of ways, not the least of which is that change in ownership is the proximate effect of the act of expropriation.

Changes in ownership of stocks, however, are not the proximate cause of economic changes in the welfare or well-being of the parties to an expropriation.[7] Rather, it is the augmentation or diminution of *flows* of services or *flows* of income (which are, in actuality, flows of generalized or nonspecific services) that increase or decrease eco-

[5] The two most notable efforts are Bronfenbrenner, *The Appeal of Confiscation in Economic Development,* 3 ECONOMIC DEVELOPMENT AND CULTURAL CHANGE 201 (1955), and A. HIRSCHMAN, HOW TO DIVEST IN LATIN AMERICA, AND WHY (1969).

[6] *See, e.g.,* Lillich, *The Valuation of Nationalized Property by the Foreign Claims Settlement Commission,* in THE VALUATION OF NATIONALIZED PROPERTY IN INTERNATIONAL LAW, *supra* note 4, at 95–116, for the views of the Commission.

[7] It may be the case that expropriation itself is the cause of changes in the political welfare of parties to the action, but here only the purely economic effects are considered.

nomic welfare. Every asset, or stock, of course, is associated with some flow of services. An automobile yields transportation services,[8] a house yields shelter, an investment yields income, *i.e.,* whatever mix of services one wishes to acquire up to the limits purchasable by the income. The flows of services generated by stocks of assets generate economic satisfaction. It is to changes in these flows, then, that one ought to look to evaluate the economic impact of an act of expropriation.

The flows of services that meet economic needs are heterogeneous. To attain comparability between flows of diverse composition it is necessary to define some *numéraire* in which these flows can be measured; the obvious *numéraire* is money. One can measure the size of any flow of services by ascertaining the amount of money that would be needed to generate an equivalent flow of services. It may be argued that the process of determining the money value of equivalent service flows is much the same as the process of determining the value of a stock via the discounted present value method, and this argument is, of course, true. But the concentration of attention on flows rather than stocks is more than a semantic difference. First, the emphasis on flows implies a rejection of all methods of asset valuation other than the discounted present value method. Second, focusing on flows directly makes it less likely that the analyst will err conceptually in his approach. Third, emphasis on flows permits the analyst to treat consistently phenomena that have different structural and methodological aspects and to generate an economically consistent definition of expropriation. Fourth, and perhaps most importantly, an emphasis on changes in flows resulting from expropriation permits an integration of the phenomenon of expropriation with international economic theory, which relies heavily on the concept of flows; this integration will be done in Section II.

A. Flows and the Discounted Present Value Method of Valuation

The first point above is rather straightforward. The concept of a flow of services implies a time dimension; the size of a flow is measured as so many units per period. Future receipts of services are subjectively valued at less than current receipts. The sum of all the future receipts of services through time, adjusted to reflect the

[8] A new automobile also yields aesthetic enjoyment and, perhaps, advertising services in that possession of a new car informs the world of the success of its owner. New cars depreciate quickly because these two services evaporate quickly; an older car yields transportation services alone.

fact that future services are currently less valuable than present services, is the present value of the stream or flow of future services. The ratio of the perceived difference in value between current and future receipt of a given service to the perceived value of current receipt of that service adjusted for units of time and the exponential effects of compounding is the discount rate, that is, the rate at which future receipts are discounted to obtain their present value equivalents.

The previous discussion is all in terms of perceived or subjective value. If money is introduced as a device for measuring and converting subjective value over time, then each potential receiver of a flow of services may translate his flow of services and his subjective time preferences into a pair of common denominators, money flows and money discount rates. If additionally a capital market exists such that some persons can exchange current for future money receipts, receiving a bonus for postponing consumption, and others can do the opposite, by paying a price, there will develop a common price for borrowers and lenders; that price will be the interest rate, or the ratio of the price paid (or received) for the use of funds to the quantity of funds used. Persons who prefer present to future receipts sufficiently that their subjective rate of discount is greater than the market rate of interest will become net borrowers. Others who discount future returns by less than the market rate of interest will become net lenders. The rate of interest will adjust so as to equate the flow of funds offered at that rate to the flow of funds borrowed at that rate.

Valuation of a stock of assets by the present value method, then, always involves recourse to the market, though it is the market for funds and not the market for commodities that is resorted to. In the event that a perfect (or nearly so) market for a particular asset exists, reference to that market for the purpose of establishing asset value will yield the same result as reference to the capital market to ascertain the present value of the money value of that asset's services, provided the flow of services is of known size, time dimension, certainty, and price. In any other case the present value method will more accurately reflect the subjective valuation of the valuor.[9]

B. Flows as a Preferred Conceptual Frame of Reference: The Weigel and Weston Analysis

Thinking about expropriation in terms of stocks tempts the analyst into conceptual error. Weigel and Weston have written a per-

[9] *See* Mintz, *supra* note 2, at 885–86.

suasive piece arguing that the proper valuation of expropriated property for the purposes of compensation is the present value of the net flow of benefits of the property to the expropriating country had the property not been taken.[10] But the peculiarity of such a position becomes apparent once it is examined in the context of flows of benefits rather than in terms of alternative valuations of stocks of assets.[11]

The benefits to the firm of the ownership of an asset abroad derive from the funds *remitted* to the home office. These funds may come from profits, as usually defined, from depreciation and depletion allowances, or from other sources such as overpayments for inputs imported from head offices. Reinvested earnings are not part of this flow;[12] they are equivalent to the postponement of present real service flows for greater future real service flows. The flow of benefits to the host country consists of value added in the production process by domestically owned resources (chiefly labor, in the case of less developed countries [LDC's]) less the opportunity cost of such resources and the income taxes received by the host country.[13] Since in most LDC's there is substantial unemployment, the opportunity cost of labor is close to zero and the wages paid labor by the firm are nearly all a net gain to the host country.

Suppose that the host country could manage the firm as well as its existing owners so that the total value added per period would

[10] Weigel & Weston, *Valuation upon the Deprivation of Foreign Enterprise: A Policy-Oriented Approach to the Problem of Compensation Under International Law,* in THE VALUATION OF NATIONALIZED PROPERTY IN INTERNATIONAL LAW, *supra* note 4, at 3–39 [hereinafter cited as WEIGEL & WESTON].

[11] It is not argued that the second approach is illegitimate; rather, it requires greater subtlety of analysis since stock valuations are second-order phenomena resulting from the evaluation of flows. Thus, this approach, by concentrating on second-order effects of changes in flows, may hide as much as it reveals about the first-order welfare implications of the flows themselves.

[12] Alternatively, they may be considered part of the benefit flow provided that new investment, which is the exchange of present benefits for expected (higher) future benefits, is subtracted in determining the net flow.

[13] Weigel and Weston deduct from this flow the difference between world and tariff-distorted domestic prices multiplied by the number of units domestically consumed per period. WEIGEL & WESTON 25. The bulk of foreign industrial investment in those countries most likely to expropriate at present, *i.e.,* the LDC's, is in export industries. Little of the product of these industries is domestically consumed. Since the host countries are efficient producers of export products (or else they could not export them), tariffs on the output of these industries tend to be low, and such domestic consumption that does take place tends to be at close to world prices. The small difference between world and domestic prices weighted by the small amount of domestic consumption may safely be ignored.

be the same if the firm were or were not expropriated. Suppose further that the firm did not reinvest any of its earnings (an assumption that will be relaxed in a moment). By expropriating the firm, the host country would increase its flow of benefits, in the absence of compensation, by the amount of benefits formerly accruing to the firm. Under the Weigel and Weston compensation standard, the expropriating country would transfer the flow of benefits that *it* had formerly received to the firm as payment.[14] Compensated expropriation would simply be an exchange of benefit flows between the host country and the expropriated firm!

If the firm had formerly reinvested part of its profits, thus changing the time dimension of its benefit flow, the country could continue this practice, or invest more or less per period. In these cases the country and the firm would be exchanging flows of potential rather than actual benefits; the analysis is the same.

Weigel and Weston observe that when the flow of benefits to the country exceeds the flow of benefits to the firm, their compensation standard will "more than compensate [the firm] for the real risks they wish to avoid and thereby encourage foreign investment in such instances."[15] But surely no country would feel obliged to pay more in compensation than the amount for which they could have *bought* the assets. If the flow of benefits to the firm is greater than that to the country, "compensation would be less than the value of the asset to the foreign investor."[16] However, it is also argued that the firm's discount rate is likely to be less than the country's discount rate.[17] If the latter contention is correct, so that a given flow will produce a higher present value for the firm than for the country, then some flow of payments over time can always be devised so as to allow the country to pay its (low) perceived value of the asset while the firm receives its (high) perceived value.[18] The confusion, of course, results from Weigel and Weston's perception of

---

[14] Weigel and Weston observe that different subjective discount rates, host country versus firm, will cause their valuations of a given flow to differ. However, see the discussion at note 18 *infra*.

[15] WEIGEL & WESTON 34.   [16] *Id.* at 35.   [17] *Id.* at 27.

[18] Suppose that the host country has a discount rate of 20% and the firm 10%. Then the present costs of $1,000 to be paid by the host country one, ten, and twenty years hence are respectively $833.33, $161.51, and $26.08. The present values of $1,000 to be received by the firm at the same points in time are $909.09, $385.54, and $148.65. The present value of a sum of money to be paid or received twenty years hence is over five times as great for the firm as for the host country! By varying the size and time dimension of the flow of compensation, then, it is possible to achieve any value of receipts to the firm consistent with any lower value of payments to the country.

value resulting from the stock of assets rather than the flow of income.

The Weigel and Weston compensation standard has another defect not related to the stock-flow analysis; account is not taken of nonmonetary benefits of foreign investment to the host country, or of nonproductive property. The latter case may be analyzed quickly. Since nonproductive property, *e.g.*, paintings, jewelry, non-agricultural land, some housing, and the like, yields no benefit flow to the host country when it is owned by foreigners, the Weigel and Weston compensation standard would suggest zero compensation for the expropriation of such property. But perhaps the case of nonproductive property is a straw man, for Weigel and Weston do not consider this case and presumably would recommend some alternative compensation standard.

The former case is more important. A large portion of foreign investment in less developed countries is in highly capital-intensive, socially desirable, overhead industries such as electric power generation, telephone systems, and railway systems. Though the direct benefits to the host country via the domestic share of value added may be low in such instances, the total benefits, including external benefits and consumer surplus, may be very high. Yet these nonmonetary benefits do not enter into the Weigel and Weston compensation scheme. Indeed, implementation of that scheme would serve as an inducement to LDC's to expropriate, and thus reduce new foreign investment in the very industries that are most necessary to the industrial base on which further development depends.

What really seems to be at issue here is the division of benefits between the host countries and the investing firms. If the country believes that the firm is engaging in activities that have external social costs, *e.g.*, pollution of air or waters, the reasonable policy for the country to follow is to legislate against such activity, or to tax the firm in the amount of the social disutility it creates. If the firm makes monopoly profits, taxation is again the answer. If the country believes the firm is earning too great a proportion of the value added in production on some ethical or other criterion (about which economists *qua* economists can have little to say), once again taxation is the simplest and most direct remedy. Taxation in these cases provides exactly the same economic remedies as physical expropriation without some of the unpleasant side effects on the international investing community.[19] If expropriation occurs, then, it

[19] In fact, additional taxation is analytically identical to expropriation provided that the host country can manage the firm as well as the firm's own managers. Otherwise taxation is preferable on efficiency grounds. *See* the discussion at note 20 *infra*.

presumably is not motivated by economic considerations alone, and any compensation agreed to by the host country will not be based solely on economic considerations. Rather the host country, the investing country, and the firm are in a monopolist-monopsonist situation with potential sanctions and countersanctions—a pure bargaining situation.

C. FLOWS AND A GENERAL DEFINITION OF EXPROPRIATION

Use of the flow approach to expropriation permits a single frame of reference to be applied to the evaluation of policy actions that are qualitatively and quantitatively similar but institutionally different. The immediate effect that expropriation of its foreign properties has on a firm (and on the investing country, for that matter) is the curtailment of the flow of funds from the host country.[20] One can devise policy actions other than simple taking of property that will have precisely the same effect as such taking on all relevant flows among all the affected parties. Among such actions are the imposition of various sorts of discriminatory taxes and transfers, foreign exchange regulations, forced sales of equity in some firms, operating and employment regulations, and, in short, any new policy that will affect the size and time dimension of income flows from the host to the investing country. Any such changes are "deprivations" in Weigel and Weston's use of the term,[21] and so are conceptually equivalent to expropriation. Expropriation itself, then, can be viewed as a policy-induced change in the rate at which, or time horizon over which, funds flow from the host country to the investing country. The foregoing definition of expropriation is implicit in the remainder of this chapter, for the specific nature of the policy action that causes a decline in the rate at which income is transferred is irrelevant for the purposes of economic analysis; the fact of the reduced flow is all that is important.

II. EXPROPRIATION AND INTERNATIONAL TRADE THEORY

This section will analyze expropriation in the frame of reference used by economists to explain welfare changes resulting from inter-

[20] Other effects might result from reactions to the expropriation, *e.g.*, curtailment of foreign aid or investment, or be in addition to expropriation, *e.g.*, refusal of the host country to sell to certain markets. These effects are separate from and must not be confused with the expropriation per se. Such effects can occur independently of expropriation.

[21] WEIGEL & WESTON 3.

national trade changes. The analysis is of a pure trade theoretic sort; there is no money in the analysis. International transfers are reflected directly by flows of goods and services.

The purpose of the analysis is to show how expropriation affects the welfare of both the host and the investing country. The analysis shows that both the direct gains and losses resulting from expropriation and the changes in the relative prices of traded goods (the barter terms of trade) affect total welfare; the cost to the United States of having its property expropriated is likely to be somewhat higher than the direct loss of repatriated earnings from subsidiaries of United States firms located abroad.

The simplifying assumptions underlying the following analysis are that each of the two countries produce and consume only two traded commodities. There are no tariffs or transport costs, nor are there increasing returns to scale. Perfect competition obtains in all markets, and there is a well-behaved community indifference set. This last assumption could be dropped without damaging the argument; it is retained for expositional convenience.

Given that residents of A, the investing country, own property located in B, the host country, there will be a flow of unrequited imports from B to A. These imports will consist of three major sorts: the direct services yield by the property (*e.g.*, houses) owned by A nationals but located in B, the consumption expenditures of A nationals working for A-owned firms located in B, and most importantly the repatriated earnings of A-owned firms located in B. Expropriation of A-owned property by the country B will cause all such flows to cease.

What is significant, in economic terms, is not the property that is taken but the flow of unrequited imports that is halted. The analysis of the effects of the cessation of such imports is identical with the analysis of other sorts of transfer problems, the large literature on which was surveyed and extended by Samuelson.[22] A simple case of expropriation is illustrated by Figure 1, based on Meade's geometry.[23]

Country A exports commodity X and imports commodity Y. Country B transfers an amount, OC, of its export good to A in each period. This amount is equal to profits earned by A investors in B, the services of consumption assets owned by A residents but located in B, and the wages of A workers employed by A-owned companies

---

[22] Samuelson, *The Transfer Problem and Transport Costs*, 62 Econ. J. 278 (1952), and 64 Econ. J. 264 (1954).

[23] J. Meade, A Geometry of International Trade 80–96 (1952).

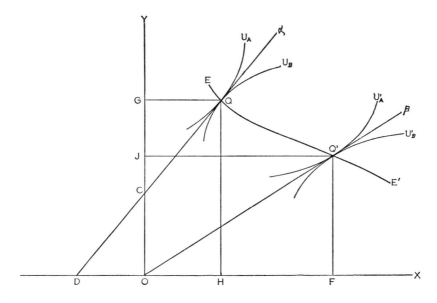

Figure 1

but domiciled in B.[24] The net barter terms of trade are represented
by the line α; OH of X exchanges for CG of Y. Line α is the marginal rate of transformation in production and the marginal rate
of substitution in consumption in both countries. The latter is
shown by the tangency of the two trade indifference curves U_A and
U_B at Q; the former is not shown. Trade takes place at point Q,
where two offer curves (not shown) originating at C intersect. Q
lies on the locus EE', which represents all points of tangency of A
and B trade indifference curves, and therefore all the efficient trade
positions of different-sized net transfers either from or to country A.

Expropriation of A-owned property in B by B's government
would mean, in the absence of compensation, the elimination of the
transfer OC formerly paid A by B. A new trade position would
occur, Q', with terms of trade β, also, of course, on EE'.[25] At this

[24] It is assumed that these workers can be repatriated without causing any
fall in the production of B goods. Perhaps there are persons in B who can take
over the functions of the repatriated A workers without causing a labor shortage
elsewhere in B. These workers may come from among those who could not
otherwise be employed in B due to institutional constraints on employment.

[25] As drawn, the new terms of trade favor the expropriating country. The necessary condition for this to occur is that the sum of the marginal propensities to
import in the two countries be less than unity. Since the marginal propensity
of the United States to import from LDC's is quite low, the condition is likely
to be met if United States–owned property is expropriated. If this condition

point, OF of X exchanges for OJ of Y. At Q' A's welfare has fallen to U'_A while B's welfare has risen to U'_B. As would be expected, expropriation without compensation enhances the welfare of the expropriating country.

The policy options available to the home country to offset its loss of welfare are two.[26] First, it may demand compensation that, to the extent that it is paid, would move the country along EE' toward the earlier position. Second, it might impose a tariff sufficient to move it back toward, or even to, U_A. Both of these may be briefly explored.

If full compensation, OC, were paid, the act of expropriation would be trivial since the trading point would move back to Q. It is highly unlikely, however, that B would pay full compensation; at the very least it would refrain from paying wages to repatriated foreigners. On recent evidence in the Chilean case, it would refuse to pay even the amount of repatriated earnings and capital depreciation, though an amount less than OC might be paid which would move Q' part of the way toward Q. But such payment is clearly against the interests of B, and we may safely assume that it will be kept to a minimum, international law notwithstanding.

Alternatively (alternatively because it is clear that no country will pay very much in the way of compensation if it is at the same time the subject of retaliatory discriminatory tariffs), country A might impose a tariff on country B. This tariff, even if it were sufficient to reach U_A, would move the system off the efficiency locus EE' and would cost B more than would the payment of full compensation. Country B might retaliate in turn, however, and both sides might end up worse than before, *i.e.*, on lower indifference curves than U'_A and U'_B. In general, the smaller the expropriating country with respect to the investing country, the less effective will be tariff retaliation by the expropriating country in restoring the pretariff terms of trade, and so the more effective the investing country's threat of tariffs will be as incentive to compensate.

We have been assuming that before the expropriation, transfers flowed only from B to A. It is likely, however, that transfers flowed in both directions, the transfer from A consisting of foreign aid and perhaps some new investment, as shown in Figure 2. The preexpropriation terms of trade would be line α with OE of Y transferred

---

were not met, Q' would be closer to Q than drawn. Q' can never be to the northwest of Q along EE' so long as unstable equilibria are ruled out. *See* Samuelson (1952), *supra* note 22, at 285–88.

[26] These options are exclusive under the assumption that there is no flow of foreign aid or investment to B; the situation is as depicted in Figure 1.

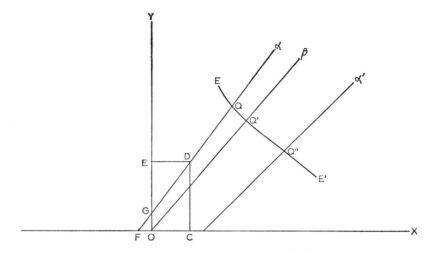

Figure 2

from B to A and OC of X transferred from A to B. As drawn, the situation augments A's income by FO measured in X or OG measured in Y. If B expropriates and no longer pays the transfer OE, A's welfare will decline along EE' to Q''. But by halting its foreign aid to and new investment in B, A can move northwest on EE' back toward Q to, say, Q'. In general Q' will always lie to the left of Q'' if multiple equilibria are prohibited.

Compensation in this case too can move the final trade position toward Q and thus improve the welfare of A. But compensation is probably incompatible with a cessation of foreign aid and investment, and so retaliation is an alternative rather than a complement to compensation. In the absence of compensation, it is always in the interest of the home country to retaliate against expropriation by eliminating transfers to the expropriating country. In this context the Hickenlooper Amendment makes perfect economic sense.[27]

III. EXPROPRIATION AND THE DISTRIBUTION
OF INCOME

The primary impact of expropriation will be felt by those (firms and individuals) in the investing country whose flow of income is

[27] Section 301 (e) of the United States Foreign Assistance Act of 1961, *as amended,* 22 U.S.C. §2370 (e) (1) (1970). For an excellent discussion of the Hickenlooper Amendment, which supports a rather different conclusion, see R. LILLICH *supra* note 1, at ch. 3.

halted. Negative secondary effects will be felt by the factor used intensively in the product whose price falls (in Figure 1 the investing country's export good *X*).

The decline in price of *X* will cause a shift in the employment of resources from *X* to *Y*. If, *e.g.*, more capital is needed per dollar of output for *X* than *Y* at all relevant factor prices (implying less labor required for *X* than *Y*), a reduction in the production of *X* will release more capital than can be absorbed by the expansion of the production of *Y* at existing factor prices. In order for this additional capital to be absorbed, there will be a decline in the rate of return to capital, which implies an increase in the relative wage rate.[28]

Although common sense is not always an accurate guide to the conclusions of economic analysis, in this case they coincide and the above point may be illustrated by analogy. Suppose a United States firm has located a shirt factory in Ruritania for the purpose of producing shirts for the United States market using Ruritanian labor and United States–owned capital. Suppose further that the United States had adjusted to this situation so that there was full employment in the United States and equilibrium in the balance of payments. If Ruritania expropriates the shirt factory, United States income will fall by the amount of previously repatriated profits. If the United States continues to demand the same quantity of shirts at the same prices as before, the United States will have to sacrifice the consumption of some other kind of goods since total United States income has fallen. If Ruritania does not use its increased income to offset fully the decline in these other goods (*X* goods in the preceding discussion), the quantity demanded of these goods will fall, their price will fall, and fewer of them will be produced. But if Ruritania does not use its higher income to absorb these other (*X*) goods, it follows that she will use that income to buy shirts, reducing the quantity that can be sold to the United States. The slack will be taken up by increased United States production of shirts. Since shirts are relatively labor-intensive, the decline in United States consumption of other (*X*) goods will not release enough labor to expand the shirt industry sufficiently at existing wage rates. Thus the shirt industry, in seeking additional labor, will bid up the wage rate, decreasing the relative return on capital, *i.e.*, the ratio of money return per unit of capital to money wages.

[28] Stolper & Samuelson, *Protection and Real Wages*, 9 REVIEW OF ECONOMIC STUDIES 58 (1941), *reprinted in* READINGS IN THE THEORY OF INTERNATIONAL TRADE (H. Ellis & L. Metzler eds. 1950).

It is worth noting that the effect that we have been discussing is one that could result from a variety of causes, *e.g.*, a change in tastes, foreign imposition of a tariff (or subsidy, depending on which way the terms of trade move), changes in tax rates, and the like. Any changes in the conditions under which trade and payments occur will have a distributional effect on the allocation of income.

Of course, any change in the flow of payments to some sector of the investing country will have primary income effects on the former recipients of the flow, and only secondary income effects on the country's factors of production; terms of trade (price) effects will be felt by the country as a whole. However, a change in the flow of payments will affect both the level and the relative distribution of income (and consumption) in the investing country.

The curious circumstance exists that a decline in the aforementioned flow does not imply an unambiguous decline in the welfare of the country as a whole, for as we have seen some groups benefit from the change, and one cannot make interpersonal utility comparisons. Only if the government were to tax the gainers by the amount of their gain and transfer this amount to the losers would a clear welfare loss result from the decline in the flow of income. Under these conditions no one would be better off than before (because all benefits had been taxed), but some (both the primary and secondary losers) would be worse off. This result requires, of course, that the distribution of income was socially optimal before the decrease in unilateral transfers. If the prior distribution of income was not optimal, the postexpropriation situation may be socially preferable.

Even if the preexpropriation distribution of income was not socially optimal, the achievement of the preexpropriation *potential* welfare level requires the reconstitution of the previous payments flow, *i.e.*, full compensation. *Ceteris paribus*, it is always in the interest of the investing country to induce such compensation, which will have precisely the reverse effect on income and income distribution as the original expropriation had. If other than full compensation via a full restoration of the income flow occurs, it constitutes an increase in the potential welfare of the expropriating country at the expense of the potential welfare of the investing country. Such changes, of course, may be desirable for the world as a whole on any number of grounds. The grounds, however, should be made explicit.[29]

[29] For example, it might be thought socially useful to tax monopoly profit accruing to the firm. This taxation would be a form of expropriation though perhaps of an unobjectionable sort. Remedies for the existence of monopoly

IV. EXTERNALITIES IN EXPROPRIATION

An act of expropriation generates effects external to the specific act, and even external to the expropriating country. These effects may be considered demonstration effects; they are of two major sorts. On the one hand other countries, potential expropriators, observe the action and resolve to do likewise. On the other hand potential investors fear, rightly or wrongly, that other countries will expropriate foreign investment and thus refrain from investing.

The first of these effects will occur even if the original expropriation effort proved to be an economic failure in the sense that the expropriated properties were mismanaged, incurred losses, and required government subsidies for their continued operation. Potential expropriators will always assume that they can do a better job of managing or can correct any other problems that might arise in the process of expropriation.

The second effect will occur even if full or nearly full compensation is paid. Potential investors will consider the compensation as a lucky windfall but feel that they might not be so lucky next time.

The incentive for other countries to imitate the expropriating country will be diminished the higher the costs the expropriating country incurs and the more certain the likelihood that they too would have to bear those costs. This calculus was the rationale of gunboat diplomacy. If the government of a potential expropriator were certain it would be overthrown and the property retaken in the event it did expropriate, the usefulness to it of an expropriation policy would be very small. The impacts of other sanctions are similar. The stronger they are and the more certain their application, the greater their deterrent effect.

Thus the ineffectiveness of the Hickenlooper Amendment as a deterrent to expropriation is explained. Though the sanction is strong, that is, the halting of foreign aid would clearly impose a heavy cost on former recipients, the probability of the occurrence of those sanctions seems to be very low. The expected cost for any country is the expected probability of the imposition of the sanction multiplied by the cost of the sanction if imposed. If the former term is near zero, of course, the expected cost is minimal. It seems

----

conditions, however justified, will reduce the welfare of the monopolist, *i.e.*, the investing country. It is argued that redistribution ought to be made explicit and evaluated on its merits. Questions of the appropriateness of policies on grounds of equity ought not be confused with questions of expropriation.

to be sufficiently low to have been disregarded in the last few years.

It is possible, of course, that no economic sanction short of warfare will prevent expropriation, as the case of Cuba shows, and in that case even the certainty of war would probably not have prevented an expropriation attempt. It is not argued that strong and certain sanctions will eliminate the first demonstration effect; only that they will lessen it.

Analogously, the second demonstration effect, the effect on investment incentives, can be lessened by home government guarantees as to the certainty and level of compensation in the event of expropriation. This, it should be noted, is not perfectly equivalent to an insurance plan in which the investors pay the government for its guarantee, such as the present United States investment guarantee program. The latter plan would generate less investment than the former (assuming guarantees at the same level) because of the increased costs incurred, and so the higher returns required, to meet the premium costs. But if continued foreign investment is desired by the home government it is better than no program at all.

V. POLICY RESPONSES TO EXPROPRIATION

The economically aggressive policies mentioned in the earlier sections of this chapter (except for discriminatory tariffs) are costly to the imposing country as well as to the country against which they are directed. (Tariffs may prove costly, too, if either they are too high or retaliation occurs.) Foreign aid, for example, presumably yields benefits to the donor as well as the recipient, or it would not continue. These benefits may be economic, moral, or political, but they are undoubtedly real. The cessation of foreign aid, then, will reduce or eliminate these benefits and may even generate additional costs by impairing relationships with third countries.

Sanctions will have different costs for the imposing country under different circumstances. For example, the costs in terms of world opinion, retaliation, and the like will be higher if a given sanction is imposed after some compensation has been paid as compared with the costs of the same sanction when no compensation has been paid. In general, it seems likely that the cost of a given level of sanctions will increase[30] with the size of compensation settlements

[30] It is tempting to write "increase at an increasing rate." But, on reflection, the sign of the rate of change of these costs is indeterminate for a variety of reasons. First, third countries may be willing to express only a limited amount

paid or promised. The costs of sanctions also will be higher the higher the level of those sanctions, holding constant the level of compensation.

Benefits gained by imposing sanctions too will increase, at least over some range, as the level of sanctions increases. Resources available for domestic consumption in the sanction-imposing country will increase as that country decreases its foreign aid; its terms of trade will improve as a result of a tariff. Either of these sorts of sanctions is likely (though not certain) to increase the total welfare of the sanction-imposing country.

The economic problem is to ascertain that level of sanctions which will generate the greatest level of welfare in the sanction-imposing country, *i.e.,* to obtain the greatest benefit net of the costs of imposing sanctions.

The economic solution is the usual one of equating marginal benefits to marginal costs. Sanctions should be increased to the point where the costs of the last increment of sanctions are equal to the benefits derived therefrom. As long as an increment of sanctions will yield a greater increase in benefits than it does in costs, it is worthwhile to impose that sanction. If the converse is true, of course, it is disadvantageous to impose additional sanctions. The dividing point between the two situations lies where marginal benefits exactly equal marginal costs.

It is possible, of course, that since both total costs and total benefits are increasing functions of the level of sanctions, total costs may always exceed total benefits for all positive levels of sanctions, *i.e.,* marginal benefit less marginal cost may always be negative. If this is the case, the optimum level of sanctions will be zero (unless negative sanctions, *e.g.,* more foreign aid or import subsidies, are permitted) .

This policy, simple as it appears, is very difficult to apply. The difficulties inhere in the required attempt to measure costs and benefits in terms of a single *numéraire,* presumably money. Quantification of essentially qualitative relationships such as international good will is a chancy business at best. Decisions are made on the basis of the evaluation of such qualitative factors, however, and it

---

of displeasure with events that do not directly concern them, and their limits may be reached at different sanction levels. Second, economic retaliation cannot proceed indefinitely; it halts when the country retaliated against becomes autarkic. Third, it is possible that some countries, perhaps ones whose own investment is in danger of expropriation, would support the country that is imposing sanctions. These countries are not likely to be so numerous as to permit costs of sanctions to be a decreasing function of their level.

seems reasonable to require decision makers to come to terms with the question of what such qualitative considerations are worth. How much is the country willing to pay for good will? Would it pay a million dollars, a hundred million, a billion? Such evaluations are always made in the decision-making process, though they are usually made implicitly. The evaluation and decision process, in principle, could be made explicit.

That the policy of equating marginal costs to marginal benefits of sanctions is not always followed in practice is evident from a cursory examination of two cases in which the United States imposed excessive sanctions. The first of these cases is Cuba. It is hard to see that the United States receives any economic benefit from the present relations (though the reaction toward Cuba may have mitigated slightly the demonstration effects of the Cuban experience). But the costs are positive and substantial—ranging from the loss of some consumption goods (Cuban cigars) to other countries' perception of the United States as a bullying giant.

In the case of Rhodesia the United States, after some lag, apparently has decided that the benefits of a moral as well as an internationally legal position do not outweigh the loss of chrome imports, and so has partially removed the embargo on trade with Rhodesia. In short, the United States itself finally deemed the previous sanctions to be excessive.

On the other side, that is, with respect to the underutilization of sanctions, it is likely, though not certain, that some sanctions would enhance the economic welfare of the United States in the de facto expropriation of former fishing rights (or, from another point of view, the assets of fishing fleet via fines) off the coast of South America, at some cost in terms of world opinion.[31]

The balancing of costs and benefits in a political as well as an economic calculus is necessary to develop optimum reactions to expropriation by those countries whose property is taken. If the goal of a government is to maximize the welfare of its residents subject to some world social constraints, it ought not to protect the property rights of its citizens when the cost of doing so is greater than the benefits. Neither, however, ought a government let its citizens absorb undesired economic welfare losses if the means for redressing those losses, at least in part, is at hand.

---

[31] It is possible that the waters off the coast of Peru are being overfished. If so, international negotiation directed toward eliminating that condition would be appropriate. If the United States yields to Peru benefits in the fishing war that she would not yield via negotiation, and that she has the power to recoup partially via retaliation, the United States is acting in an irrational way.

CHAPTER III

Book Values in
Nationalization Settlements

Joseph S. McCosker

IS BOOK VALUE a fair value for settling nationalization claims? Do "generally accepted principles of accounting" in the United States provide a basis for settling such claims that is equitable both to the expropriating state and to the person whose property is expropriated?[1] These questions are examined in this chapter.

The chapter begins with a definition of book value and related terms as used by accountants, followed by a discussion of generally accepted principles of accounting in the United States, a review of certain concepts underlying those principles, and an explanation of the "pervasive principles" of accounting. Then a typical balance sheet of a nationalized company is examined in order to determine the fairness of the use of book values in settling nationalization claims.

Accountants use the term *book value* in two different ways. Book value means the amount at which a particular item appears in the books of account. Book value also is used to refer to the value on the books of account of the owners' equity in an enterprise. Owners' equity is the amount that remains after deducting the liabilities from the assets of a company in the amounts that these items appear on the company's books of account. Book value in this sense can be presented in equation form:

$$\text{Book value} = \text{total assets} - \text{total liabilities.}$$

This second use of the term *book value,* as the amount of owners' equity, is the meaning that is used in connection with nationalization settlements. If a nationalization claim is settled on the basis of book value, then the claimant is awarded the amount of owners' equity as shown on the books of the company. However, the first

---

[1] Fair value, to which book value is compared in this chapter, is assumed to be the fair market value of the nationalized property at the time and place of the nationalization. "Fair market value is generally designated as the price a willing buyer would pay a willing seller at the time of the loss, uninfluenced by the circumstance of state interference." Smith, *Real Property Valuation for Foreign Wealth Deprivations,* in THE VALUATION OF NATIONALIZED PROPERTY IN INTERNATIONAL LAW 141 (R. Lillich ed. & contrib. 1972).

definition of book value is also relevant. Looking at the above equation, it can be seen that book value:

is increased by an increase in assets;
is decreased by a decrease in assets;
is decreased by an increase in liabilities;
is increased by a decrease in liabilities.

Also:

If assets are overstated, then book value is greater than the fair value of a company.

If assets are understated, then book value is less than the fair value of a company.

If liabilities are overstated, then book value is less than the fair value of a company.

If liabilities are understated, then book value is greater than the fair value of a company.

Consequently, book value depends on the amounts assigned to assets and liabilities. It is appropriate, therefore, to examine how accountants define these terms.

Accountants define *assets* as "economic resources of an enterprise that are recognized and measured in conformity with generally accepted accounting principles."[2] *Liabilities* are "economic obligations of an enterprise that are recognized and measured in conformity with generally accepted accouting principles."[3] Other relevant terms used by accountants are *revenue, expenses,* and *net income.*

Revenue refers to "gross increases in assets or gross decreases in liabilities recognized and measured in conformity with generally accepted accounting principles that result from those types of profit-directed activities of an enterprise that can change owners' equity."[4] Common examples of revenues are sales of products and services, interest income, dividend income, and rental income.

Expenses are "gross decreases in assets or gross increases in liabilities recognized and measured in conformity with generally accepted accounting principles that result from those types of profit-directed activities of an enterprise that can change owners' equity."[5]

Net income is equal to revenues minus expenses of an enterprise for an accounting period.

[2] AICPA, Basic Concepts and Accounting Principles Underlying Financial Statements of Business Enterprises, Accounting Principles Board Statement No. 4 ¶ 132 (1970) (Copyright © 1970 by the American Institute of Certified Public Accountants, Inc.) [hereinafter cited as Statement No. 4].

[3] *Id.*   [4] *Id.* ¶ 134.   [5] *Id.*

These definitions are keyed to the phrase "in conformity with generally accepted accounting principles." Therefore, in order to appraise the fairness of book values in settling nationalization claims, it is necessary to look at generally accepted accounting principles.

I. GENERALLY ACCEPTED ACCOUNTING PRINCIPLES IN THE UNITED STATES

To many people, the word *principle* connotes "[a] fundamental truth; a comprehensive law or doctrine, from which others are derived, or on which others are founded."[6] Accountants have used the word in a less basic sense; in accounting a principle is not so much a fundamental truth as it is a way of conceiving or of practicing matters related to accounting that have found general acceptance by the accounting profession. The definition that probably comes nearest to describing what most accountants mean by the word *principle* is: " 'A general law or rule adopted or professed as a guide to action; a settled ground or basis of conduct or practice. . . .' "[7]

The phrase "generally accepted principles" includes not only broad guidelines of general application but also detailed practices and procedures. In the past three decades there have been various attempts to specify and agree upon these principles. However, there still is no comprehensive code of accounting principles that has been accepted by United States accountants. The most authoritative set of accounting principles are the Opinions of the Accounting Principles Board [APB] of the American Institute of Certified Public Accountants [AICPA]. The AICPA is the national professional organization of Certified Public Accountants in the United States. The APB is the senior technical body of the AICPA authorized to issue pronouncements on accounting principles.[8] In 1970, the APB

[6] WEBSTER'S NEW INTERNATIONAL DICTIONARY OF THE ENGLISH LANGUAGE (2d ed. W. Neilson ed. 1961).

[7] AICPA COMMITTEE ON TERMINOLOGY, ACCOUNTING TERMINOLOGY BULLETIN No. 1 ¶ 16 (1953) (Copyright © 1953 by the American Institute of Certified Public Accountants, Inc.).

[8] In March 1971 the AICPA President appointed a Study Group to review the organization and operation of the APB and to make suggestions for improvement. The Study Group recommended in March 1972 that the APB be replaced by a broad-based organization including a new Financial Accounting Standards Board to establish accounting principles. This recommendation was approved by the Board of Directors of the AICPA in April 1972 and by the Council of the AICPA in May 1972. It is expected that the APB will continue to operate until early 1973 and then be superseded by the Financial Accounting Standards Board. Nevertheless, the pronouncements of the APB will remain in effect unless they are specifically changed by the Financial Accounting Standards Board.

issued *Basic Concepts and Accounting Principles Underlying Financial Statements of Business Enterprises, Accounting Principles Board Statement No. 4.* This publication was issued as a "Statement" and does not have the authority of an APB Opinion. Nevertheless, it is the most authoritative description of accounting principles as they exist today and therefore is used as a framework for discussion in this chapter. The discussion begins in the next section with an explanation of some of the concepts underlying accounting principles and is followed in the subsequent section with an examination of the "pervasive principles" of accounting.

II. THE PROBLEM OF UNCERTAINTY

Companies issue balance sheets and income statements at periodic intervals—yearly, quarterly, or even more frequently—during the life of an enterprise. In preparing these financial statements, accountants have to make judgments about the future of the enterprise so that they can value certain assets and liabilities at the balance sheet date and assign revenues and expenses to allocable periods. These judgments involve answers to questions such as: What future benefits will be received from the company's plant and equipment and in what future periods will they be received? How will the value of the company's inventory be affected by changes in demand for its product? What future benefits, if any, will be received from expenditures made for research and development?

No crystal ball has been found that will give precise answers to the above questions. In order to satisfy the need to issue periodic financial statements before final answers to such questions are available, accountants have had to develop concepts to enable them to operate under conditions of uncertainty. It is useful to examine these concepts since they provide the rationale for many of the accounting principles. Particularly important are the concepts of verifiability, going concern, and conservatism.[9]

A. VERIFIABILITY

Verifiability means that results shown on financial statements "would be substantially duplicated by independent measurers using the same measurement methods."[10] It means that accountants prefer

[9] STATEMENT No. 4 refers to the concepts of verifiability, going concern, and conservatism. However, the grouping of these concepts under "The Problem of Uncertainty" was made by the author.

[10] STATEMENT No. 4 ¶ 90.

to measure assets and liabilities by methods based on "objective evidence," that is, "evidence that is sufficiently clear cut that reasonable men will vary in their interpretation of it only within fairly narrow limits."[11]

Although no one would argue that accounting measurements should not be verifiable, a problem arises in that sometimes a measurement method may be verifiable but it will produce biased results. Suppose that in 1951 a company acquired 100 acres of land at a cost of $100,000. On December 31, 1971, the land was appraised by three qualified appraisers who developed estimates of $900,000, $1,000,000, and $1,100,000, respectively. At this date the original cost of $100,000 was verifiable since accountants working independently could examine documentary evidence and arrive at the same figure. Appraisal estimates rank low in verifiability, as shown by the variation among the three estimates. Because accountants prefer measurement methods that are verifiable they would value the land at its original cost although any one of the appraisal estimates probably would be closer to its fair value at December 31, 1971.

B. Going Concern Assumption

Balance sheets are prepared on the assumption that a company will continue in business, that it will be a "going concern." If accountants did not use this assumption, reported financial results would be subject to wide fluctuations that would not necessarily reflect the expectations of a particular enterprise.

Accountants' valuation of partially completed inventory, commonly called "work in process," provides an illustration of the going concern assumption. At the balance sheet date a manufacturing company may own an inventory of partially completed machinery that was produced at substantial cost. Without the going concern assumption the machinery in process of manufacture would be worth only scrap value. Using the going concern assumption, work in process can be valued on the premise that the work will be completed and sold as finished articles.

The going concern assumption means that a company is considered to continue in operation in the absence of evidence to the contrary. If liquidation of the company appears imminent, then the

---

[11] W. Meigs, C. Johnson, T. Keller & A. Mosich, Intermediate Accounting 72 (2d ed. 1968).

going concern assumption is not used, and assets and liabilities are valued on a basis that is relevant to that company.

C. Conservatism

In measuring assets and liabilities under conditions of uncertainty, accountants have employed the "modifying convention" of conservatism. It is thought that measurement errors that overstate assets or understate liabilities are more dangerous to the owners and creditors of a business than errors in the opposite direction. The consequences of losses, cessation of dividend payments, and bankruptcy are more serious than the consequences of unexpected profits. Therefore, when dealing with uncertainty accountants tend to be conservative. Facing a choice, they will use a lower valuation for assets and a higher valuation for liabilities. Also, conservatism implies that profits will not be recorded until they are relatively certain, but that losses will be recognized early in the accounting process. Conservatism is not a license for deliberate understatement of assets or profits or overstatement of losses or liabilities; rather, it is an accepted concept for dealing with situations involving uncertainty.

The concept of conservatism dates to an earlier time when much of the work of accountants was preparation of balance sheets for creditors who preferred to minimize their risks by using statements prepared on a conservative basis. However, conservatism introduces a bias that understates the value of an enterprise and therefore is prejudiced against an owner who sells his interest for book value.

III. PERVASIVE PRINCIPLES

Statement No. 4 defines pervasive principles as those principles "which relate to financial accounting as a whole and provide a basis for the other principles."[12] Knowledge of the pervasive principles, which are explained below, is sufficient to provide a general understanding of the fairness of generally accepted principles of accounting as a basis for settling nationalization claims. The other principles, known as broad operating principles and detailed accounting principles, are derived from the pervasive principles and are set forth in *Statement No. 4*.

[12] Statement No. 4 ¶ 141.

A. Initial Recording of Assets and
Liabilities and Revenue Recognition

The most important accounting principles insofar as nationalization settlements are concerned are those dealing with the initial recording of assets and liabilities and with revenue recognition.

Assets are first recorded at the "exchange price" at which one accounting entity[13] acquires assets from another entity. The exchange price is the amount of money paid for the assets or, if the exchange does not involve money, the fair value of the assets given up or of the assets acquired, whichever is more clearly evident.

Liabilities are initially recorded at the "exchange price" at which a company incurs obligations to another company. The theoretical value of the obligation at the balance sheet date is the present value[14] of the amount that will have to be paid to discharge the obligation. However, most current liabilities are not discounted to their present values because the discount period is short and the amount of discount is not significant. On the other hand, long-term liabilities generally are recorded at their present values when the obligations are incurred. Long-term liabilities include obligations such as bonds payable, notes payable, and contractual obligations for purchase of plant and equipment.[15]

How does a company measure changes in value of assets and liabilities? Revenues, changes that increase the value of assets or decrease the value of liabilities, are discussed below. In the next section expenses, decreases in the value of assets or increases in the value of liabilities, are considered.

From an economic point of view, all the productive activities

---

[13] "In financial accounting, the entity is the specific business enterprise. . . . The boundaries of the accounting entity may not be the same as those of the legal entity, for example, a parent corporation and its subsidiaries [may be] treated as a single business enterprise." *Id.* at ¶ 116.

[14] Present value is the value at the present date of all future payments (both principal and interest) under an obligation discounted at an appropriate rate of interest.

[15] Assets and liabilities that are classified as "current" are summarized separately from other assets and liabilities on the balance sheet. Current assets consist of cash and other assets that are reasonably expected to be: (a) realized in cash or (b) consumed during the normal operating cycle of the business or within one year, whichever is longer. Current liabilities are those expected to be satisfied: (a) by the use of current assets or the creation of other current liabilities, or (b) within one year. Liabilities other than current liabilities are referred to as "noncurrent" or "long-term" liabilities.

of a business add value to an enterprise. Research and development, production, transportation, storage, and marketing activities are all part of a process intended to increase the value of a company's assets. However, accountants do not recognize value added as each part in the process is performed because: (a) it is not possible to verify how much value is attributable to each stage in the process, and (b) there is a risk that an anticipated increase in value will not be realized because the products will not be sold at the anticipated price or because total costs will exceed estimates. In other words, accountants do not add value as each part in the process is performed because of the underlying concepts of verifiability and conservatism. Accountants require that both of the following conditions must be met before revenue is recognized in the accounts: (a) the earnings process must be complete or virtually complete, and (b) an exchange with another accounting entity must have taken place. In general, these conditions mean that revenue is recognized only when assets are sold or services are rendered to independent third parties.[16]

The combination of the rules regarding initial recording of assets and recognition of revenues is the basis for the "cost principle," which is sometimes described as the "historical cost rule." In general, an entity must report assets on the balance sheet at their historical cost (acquisition cost) even though current fair values may be substantially in excess of historical cost.

B. Expenses

While revenues result in increases in assets or decreases in liabilities, expenses produce decreases in assets or increases in liabilities. *Statement No. 4* lists three principles for recognizing the expenses to be deducted from revenues to determine net income for a particular accounting period. These principles are known as "associating cause and effect," "systematic and rational allocation," and "immediate recognition."[17]

---

[16] Under certain circumstances revenue may be recognized before the required conditions are met. Revenue may be recorded at the completion of production of certain products that have a fixed selling price and insignificant marketing costs. Revenue from cost-plus-fixed-fee and long-term construction contracts may be recognized as work progresses using the percentage-of-completion method if reasonable estimates can be made of total cost and of the ratio of work done to total work to be performed under the contract, and if collection of the contract price is reasonably assured. STATEMENT No. 4 ¶¶ 150–52, 184.

[17] *Id.* ¶ 156.

Costs are examined first to ascertain whether there is a direct association between particular costs and specific revenues. For example, costs of products sold and sales commissions can be directly identified with specific sales.

If costs cannot be associated with specific revenues, an attempt is made to associate costs with particular accounting periods in a systematic and rational manner. Examples of such costs and the related allocations to expense are: plant assets are depreciated over their expected useful life; patents and copyrights are amortized over their expected economic life or legal life, whichever is shorter; and prepaid rent is allocated to expense in equal amounts each period.

Some costs cannot be associated with revenues or will provide no discernible benefits in future periods. Such costs are given immediate recognition as expenses in the period in which the costs are incurred. Most administrative and selling costs are of this nature. The principle of immediate recognition also applies to assets carried forward from prior periods for which it is expected that there will be no future benefits, such as research and development costs on discontinued projects.

C. Unit of Measure

Another pervasive accounting principle is that "[t]he U.S. dollar is the unit of measure in financial accounting in the United States. Changes in its general purchasing power are not recognized in the basic financial statements."[18] As a result of this principle, in periods of continued inflation balance sheet amounts tend to understate the value of long-lived assets in terms of dollars of constant purchasing power.

D. Modifying Conventions

Strict adherence to the pervasive principles may be undesirable or impractical in certain circumstances. In these instances the pervasive principles are moderated by applying the "modifying conventions" of conservatism, emphasis on income, or application of judgment by the accounting profession as a whole.[19]

Conservatism was discussed as one of the accountants' methods of

[18] *Id.* ¶ 166.   [19] *Id.* ¶¶ 169–74.

dealing with uncertainty. The "lower of cost or market" method of inventory pricing is an illustration of conservatism as a modifying convention. In accordance with the applicable pervasive principle, inventory costs are associated with sales during the period and with goods still on hand in order to calculate the expense of goods sold and the value of goods remaining in inventory at the end of the period. Because of conservatism, the ending inventory valuation based on cost is then compared to market prices at the balance sheet date and revalued on the lower of cost or market basis. Suppose, for example, that a company has in inventory 1,000,000 pounds of copper that cost sixty cents a pound but that market price has fallen to fifty cents a pound at the end of the year. Cost is $600,000 and market value $500,000; the lower of cost or market rule requires that the book value of the inventory be reduced to $500,000. Suppose further that the company still owns the 1,000,000 pounds of copper at the end of the following year and that the market price of copper has increased to sixty-five cents a pound. Cost of the inventory is $600,000, book value $500,000, and market value $650,000. Because of conservatism, the book value of the inventory must remain at $500,000 even though that value is below cost and below market value.

Accounting principles are sometimes modified to produce a more meaningful income statement even though the resulting effect on the balance sheet may be undesirable. For example, the calculation of depreciation of plant and equipment is intended to allocate the cost of those items to expense in a systematic and rational manner. Yet the book value of plant and equipment on the balance sheet (cost less accumulated depreciation) at any time after the acquisition date does not correspond to its fair value, nor is there any attempt to make it equal fair value. Also, the last-in, first-out method of inventory valuation has been developed to produce a better measure of income in periods of inflation. Although this method reduces the effect of inflation on the income statement, it results in even lower amounts on the balance sheet, so that in periods of inflation inventory valuations tend to be substantially understated.

The last modifying convention, application of judgment by the accounting profession as a whole, means that in instances where rigid adherence to the pervasive principles produces results that are considered to be unreasonable or possibly misleading, the principles may be set aside in favor of other methods favored by the accounting profession as a whole. This technique is "a means of substituting the collective judgment of the profession for that of the individual accountant" in those instances.[20] These situations are relatively few in number but can be important to a particular company.

The effect of the modifying conventions on book values can be summarized as follows: Conservatism imparts a downward bias to book values, emphasis on income tends to produce meaningless book values on the balance sheets, and application of judgment by the profession as a whole gives results that may increase or decrease book values depending on the particular situation.

IV. BOOK VALUES AND A NATIONALIZED COMPANY

Let us examine the balance sheet of a hypothetical foreign subsidiary of a United States corporation that has just been nationalized (Exhibit 1). The host country offers to compensate the foreign parent company for the book value of its subsidiary, which in this case is $213,000,000 (total stockholders' equity). To ascertain the fairness of this settlement it is necessary to look at the valuation of assets and liabilities on the balance sheet, inasmuch as stockholders' equity is merely the residual of total assets less total liabilities of the subsidiary.

A. ASSETS

The first group of items on the balance sheet is current assets. The item "Cash" comprises cash on hand and in banks at the balance sheet date. Accounts receivable are valued at the total of the amounts to be collected less an estimated allowance for amounts that will be uncollectible. Since the accounts receivable generally are not due until after the balance sheet date, they are worth only the present value of the amounts that will be collected and therefore are overstated on the balance sheet. However, the amount of the overstatement normally is relatively small because the discount period is short. Moreover, some of the current liabilities also are not discounted to their present value. Thus, the overstatement of accounts receivable tends to be offset by an overstatement of current liabilities, and the net effect on book value of owners' equity generally is not significant.

Inventories, usually the largest item of current assets, are likely

---

[20] *Id.* ¶ 170.

Exhibit I. FOREIGN SUBSIDIARY BALANCE SHEET, December 31, 1971

Assets		
Current assets		
Cash		$ 2,000,000
Accounts receivable, net of allowance for		
uncollectible accounts of $100,000		7,000,000
Inventories		33,000,000
Prepaid expenses		3,000,000
Total current assets		$ 45,000,000
Property, plant, and equipment		
Buildings, machinery, and equipment, at		
cost less accumulated depreciation of		
$50,000,000		$125,000,000
Mines and mining claims, at cost less		
accumulated depletion of $25,000,000		75,000,000
		$200,000,000
Expenditures for mine development, at cost		88,000,000
Intangible assets		5,000,000
Total assets		$338,000,000

Liabilities and Stockholders' Equity		
Current liabilities		
Accounts payable		$ 5,500,000
Taxes payable		4,000,000
Payable to parent company		10,000,000
Other current liabilities		5,500,000
Total current liabilities		$ 25,000,000
Bonds payable, 6%, due December 31, 1981		100,000,000
Stockholders' equity		
Capital stock		50,000,000
Additional paid-in capital		75,000,000
Retained earnings		88,000,000
Total stockholders' equity		213,000,000
Total liabilities and stockholders' equity		$338,000,000

to be stated at less than fair value, may be stated at the equivalent of fair value, but certainly are not stated at more than fair value because of the lower of cost or market rule. If inventories are priced under the last-in, first-out method, and if there has been a significant increase in prices since inventories were first acquired, then balance sheet valuation will be significantly less than the current fair value of inventories.

Prepaid expenses generally consist of items such as prepaid rent, taxes, and insurance and are included in the balance sheet at amounts approximating their fair values on a going concern basis.

The book value of total current assets generally will be less than their fair value because of the undervaluation of inventories.

In the next group of assets, buildings, machinery, and equipment are valued at historical cost less accumulated depreciation. In periods of sustained inflation, historical cost is likely to be less than fair value of these assets. Accumulated depreciation does not necessarily bear any relation to the loss in fair value of buildings, machinery, and equipment during the time that they were used by the company, but rather represents the sum of the depreciation calculations made in connection with the computation of income. As a result, book values of these assets may be greater or less than their fair values; only by coincidence would the two values be equal.

The next two items, mines and mining claims and expenditures for mine development, pertain to companies in extractive industries. These companies make substantial investments in searching for mineral deposits and in building production, transportation, and marketing facilities. Book value is not fair value for mining properties that are nationalized because:

1. If a company should discover valuable mineral resources and then be nationalized on the basis of book value it would recover only its cost, whereas if a company should be unsuccessful in its exploration the host country would not nationalize that investment but would let the foreign company stand the loss. It is a "heads-I-win-tails-you-lose" policy that is biased against the foreign company.

2. Book value normally excludes interest on an investment prior to its use. There may be a long period of development and construction of facilities during which a company will invest substantial sums before revenue is received from the investment. Interest on the investment during this period is an economic cost, and failure to include such interest results in understatement of assets.

3. Book value is based on historical cost, which does not take into account changes in the general purchasing power of the United States dollar. Since book value is stated in terms of dollars, it under-

states these assets (mines, mining claims, and mine development) in periods of inflation.

The classification "Intangible assets" includes such items as patents, copyrights, research and development, trademarks, and good will. Intangible assets are valued at historical cost or at cost less an accumulated amortization allowance. Because of conservatism items are removed from the asset accounts when they cease to have value, but items that have increased in value continue to be shown at cost. Therefore, these assets may be materially undervalued on the balance sheet. Patents, research and development, and other such items may produce future benefits substantially in excess of their cost on the books of account.

Good will is a special type of intangible asset that reflects such factors as favorable attitudes of customers, good relations with employees, superior management, or a particularly desirable location. A company demonstrates evidence of good will when its rate of return on owners' equity is in excess of a normal rate.

Under generally accepted principles of accounting, good will is included on a balance sheet only when it is purchased. If a business purchases another company for a price that exceeds the value of its identifiable assets, the excess amount is deemed to be the cost of good will and is valued at cost less amortization. Good will must be amortized over its estimated useful life or forty years, whichever is shorter, even though a company may currently make expenditures to maintain the value of good will.

A company also may generate good will through its own activities: expenditures and policies to obtain favorable customer relations, development of a loyal work force, recruitment and training of outstanding management personnel, and other such factors. Although internally generated good will may have substantial real value, it is not shown on the balance sheet because, in the absence of an exchange transaction with another company, it does not meet the accountant's test of verifiability. Omission or understatement of good will may result in the substantial undervaluation of a nationalized company.

B. Liabilities

In general, current liabilities are shown on the balance sheet at their approximate fair values. The tendency to overstate current liabilities was described above in connection with current assets.

The foreign subsidiary has a long-term liability—6 percent bonds payable due in ten years totaling $100,000,000. This amount reflects the market rate of interest at the time that the bonds were issued. Accountants do not change book values of long-term liabilities to reflect subsequent changes in market rates of interest. As a result, book values of long-term liabilities may vary from their market values. If the market rate of interest increases, bond prices should fall, and liabilities on the balance sheet would be greater than the present value of the obligation. If the market rate of interest decreases, bond prices should rise, and liabilities on the balance sheet would be less than the present value of the obligation. Suppose that market interest rates for bonds of this risk class should rise to 7 percent; the market value of the 6 percent bonds would fall from $100,000,000 to $92,894,000. If interest rates drop to 5 percent, then the market value of the bonds would increase to $107,795,000. In both instances the balance sheet liability would continue at $100,-000,000.

The difference between book values and fair market values of long-term liabilities may be significant to some companies; but it is likely to be less important than the difference between book values and fair market values of assets, both because assets involve larger amounts and because of the many factors that tend to understate asset values.

C. Contingent Assets and Contingent Liabilities

In addition to the assets and liabilities that are shown on the balance sheet and reflected in book value of owners' equity, a company may have "contingent assets" or "contingent liabilities." These items are assets or liabilities whose existence or value depends upon the happening of a future event.

A common example of a contingent asset is a claim calling for payment of damages to the company that is in litigation at the balance sheet date. A pending lawsuit calling for payment of damages by the company is a contingent liability. Contingent assets and contingent liabilities generally are not included in balance sheet totals but are disclosed in notes to the balance sheet.

Problems of contingent assets and contingent liabilities of nationalized companies can be resolved by excluding these items from the nationalization claim and by providing that the foreign subsidiary or its parent will receive the rights to acquire contingent assets or will assume responsibility for satisfying contingent liabilities.

V. CONCLUSION

Generally accepted principles of accounting result in book values that normally are less than the fair values of the assets of nationalized companies. In a few instances the book value is greater than the fair value of a company's assets.

Most liabilities are fairly stated on company balance sheets. However, changes in interest rates may result in overstatement or understatement of long-term liabilities.

Contingent assets and contingent liabilities are not included in balance sheet totals, although they may be significant to a particular company. These items can be treated separately so that they do not present a valuation problem in settling nationalization claims.

Overall, generally accepted principles of accounting result in a book value of owners' equity that usually is less than fair value, occasionally is greater than fair value, and only by coincidence is equal to fair value. Book value is not intended to be an equitable basis for settling nationalization claims and should not be used for that purpose.

Contemporary International Practice

Days of Revindication and National Dignity: Petroleum Expropriations in Peru and Bolivia

Dale B. Furnish

PERU and Bolivia, neighbors by geography and culture, have a history that runs parallel and often intertwines. In 1839, for a short time, the young republics joined in an unsuccessful alliance under a single constitution.[1] In 1879 they fought together and lost to Chile in the War of the Pacific.[2] Most recently they have, within about a year of each other, taken action against large foreign oil companies by expropriating the property of Standard Oil's Peruvian subsidiary, International Petroleum Company (IPC), and the Bolivian Gulf Oil Company (BOGOC). The circumstances and events surrounding the expropriations in the two countries are remarkably similar on their surface.

In early October 1968, in the midst of debate over a final settlement of the long-standing La Brea y Pariñas controversy, a military coup deposed the popularly elected president of Peru. A few days later, in its first act of major importance, the new government ordered military occupation of IPC's installations in the disputed field, proclaiming a Day of National Dignity and citing revindication of the national patrimony as the legal basis for its action.[3]

---

[1] 2 J. BASADRE, HISTORIA DE LA REPUBLICA DEL PERU 99–183 (6th ed. 1968).

[2] *Id.* at vol. 8.

[3] A number of publications deal with the La Brea y Pariñas controversy. Esso Inter-America has published three volumes of English translations of the primary sources. THE LA BREA Y PARIÑAS CONTROVERSY (1969) [hereinafter cited as CONTROVERSY]. Selections from these materials have appeared in 7 INT'L LEGAL MATERIALS 1201 (1968) and 8 INT'L LEGAL MATERIALS 264 (1969). Under IPC's auspices, the following books were published: L. ECHECOPAR, INFORME JURÍDICO SOBRE EL CASO DE LA BREA Y PARIÑAS (1960); E. ELEJALDE, J. GALVEZ AYARZA, J. DEL BUSTO & A. DE COSSIO, LAUDO ARBITRAL DE LA BREA Y PARIÑAS (1963); E. ELEJALDE, J. GALVEZ AYARZA, J. DEL BUSTO, A. DE COSSIO & J. DEL SOLAR, LA BREA Y PARIÑAS: EXAMEN JURÍDICO DE LOS PROYECTOS DE LEY PRESENTADOS EN EL PARLAMENTO (1963); LONDON & PACIFIC PETROLEUM CO., HISTORIA DE LA BREA Y PARIÑAS (2d ed. 1960); A. OSORES, M. VILLARAN, H. VALLADÂO, L. CARNEIRO & L. ECHECOPAR, LA BREA Y PARIÑAS: DISCURSOS ANTE EL SENADO (LEGISLATURA EXTRAORDINARIA DE 1917) Y DICTAMENES JURÍDICOS (1963). Other publications relating to the case include R. ZIMMERMAN, LA HISTORIA SECRETA DEL PETROLEO (1968); a series of five studies by Castañeda for a Senate Special Commission charged with "studying and giving an opinion over all matters concerning the

In late September 1969, Bolivia's constitutional president was engaged in renegotiating BOGOC's concession agreement when he was overthrown by his Chief of the Armed Forces. The new government first invalidated the petroleum laws under which Gulf Oil held its concession. Then, after noting that the Bolivian "revolution is fundamentally the same as Peru's,"[4] the new de facto president sent police and army units to take over BOGOC's offices and field installations. The date was decreed a Day of National Dignity, and revindication was a term frequently used in justifying the act.[5]

The outward similarities in the course of events in Peru and Bolivia seem almost too strong to be coincidental. Before one begins to suspect a plot against foreign oil companies, let the author hasten to point out that, as in many cases of Latin American events,

---

La Brea y Pariñas question," as follows: Castañeda, *Análisis del Laudo que Pretendió Poner Término a la Controversia sobre "La Brea y Pariñas,"* 28 REVISTA DE DERECHO Y CIENCIAS POLÍTICAS 5 (1964); *La Anticonstitucionalidad de la Ley No. 3016, y la Cuestión de "La Brea y Pariñas,"* 22 REVISTA DE JURISPRUDENCIA PERUANA 364 (1964); *La Doctrina del Registro de la Propiedad Inmueble: La Revisión Internacional Ordenada por Ley,* 22 *id.* 871 (1964); *La Prescripción en la Consolidación del Dominio sobre "La Brea y Pariñas" No Ha Funcionado,* 21 *id.* 1574 (1963); and *Análisis del Derecho de Propiedad sobre "La Brea y Pariñas,"* 50 REVISTA DEL FORO 1 (1963) [hereinafter cited as Castañeda, *Propiedad*]; Goodwin, *Letter from Peru,* NEW YORKER, May 17, 1969, at 41; Furnish, *Peruvian Domestic Law Aspects of the La Brea y Pariñas Controversy,* 89 KY. L.J. 351 (1970); Zárate Polo, *Impugnación a la Tesis de la International Petroleum Company sobre la Propiedad Absoluta que Se Atribuye, del Subsuelo y de los Yacimientos Petrolíferos de "La Brea y Pariñas,"* 18 REVISTA DE JURISPRUDENCIA PERUANA 458, 482 (1960). This list is not exhaustive; Peruvian law reviews and journals over the last decade have included a number of articles related to the controversy, and several other books on it have been published in Peru.

Perhaps two unpublished sources should also be cited as excellent treatments of the subject: S. Lewis, The International Petroleum Company vs. Peru: A Case Study in Nationalism, Management and International Relations, April 1972 (unpublished manuscript, California State College at Hayward) [hereinafter cited as Case Study]; G. Treverton, Politics and Petroleum: The International Petroleum Company in Peru, April 1969 (unpublished senior thesis in Princeton University Library).

[4] W. Radmann, Nationalization in Bolivia: Gulf Oil Investments, Negotiation Patterns and Settlement Agreements, 1972, at 23 (unpublished manuscript, Texas Southern University) [hereinafter cited as Radmann, Nationalization in Bolivia].

[5] The materials concerning Gulf Oil in Bolivia are less voluminous, although the author is unfamiliar with Bolivian sources and may thus have missed many. *See* Lumpkin, *Gulf Oil's Experience in Bolivia,* 8 HOUSTON L. REV. 472, 478 (1971); the official acts and documents published in 8 INT'L LEGAL MATERIALS 1163 (1969), 10 *id.* 1–5, 94–127, 173–88, 1113–51, 1201–23 (1971); Radmann, Nationalization in Bolivia.

the superficial similarities hide profound differences in the history, the politics, and the law of the two petroleum nationalizations. This chapter will attempt to analyze and explain these basic differences in background and impact. Primary emphasis will be placed on the legal aspects of the expropriations. Peru will receive more attention than Bolivia here, in part because the author is more familiar with Peruvian events. More importantly, however, the IPC controversy in Peru is one of much greater substance and complexity than that of BOGOC. There was no compensation to IPC by Peru and no immediate prospect for any; an indemnity agreement was accepted by both sides in the BOGOC expropriation in less than a year. The latter may then be characterized as a simple political maneuver — and not overly successful at that, since its perpetrator is no longer in power — with little justification in law, economics, or good sense. Peru's controversy with IPC over La Brea y Pariñas may have elements of the same considerations that went into Bolivia's decision to nationalize BOGOC, but whereas the BOGOC affair probably can be characterized with reasonable accuracy in a sentence as simple as the one preceding this, the IPC case probably never will be analyzed definitively regardless of the words devoted to it.

The story of the La Brea y Pariñas oil field dates at least from the time of the Incas, when pitch was taken from surface flows. Pitch-collecting operations continued under Spanish rule and during the early days of the Peruvian Republic. It was at La Brea y Pariñas that the Peruvian Genaro Helguero, an early oil promoter whose family owned the hacienda that later became IPC's oil field, used Colonel Drake's process and helped to dig the first oil well in South America.[6] When Helguero's initiative paid off with a viable petroleum field which he was able to sell to foreign investors, the stage was set for a confrontation years later. Such disparate elements as the following have all played key roles: a law signed in 1825 by Simón Bolívar to facilitate payment of debts incurred by Peru in the revolutionary effort, a title to a "pitch mine" issued a year later under that law, executive decrees that purported to settle the nature and extent of the petroleum resources in 1887 and 1888, an international arbitration award of 1922, and the process of evolution and definition of a special legal regime for petroleum rights and exploitation in Peru. One of the complicating factors in the La Brea y Pariñas controversy has been the insistence of its participants on attempting to serve law and history rather than making a clean, if arbitrary and subjective, break with the past. Thus history and

---

[6] *See* Lewis, Case Study 7.

law are essential to understanding Peru's nationalization without compensation.

Bolivia's case is simpler because it has been willing to pay for making a clean break, not once but twice. The first nationalization of a North American petroleum interest in Latin America occurred in Bolivia in 1937, when Standard Oil's sixteen-year-old concession was terminated by President David Toro. After a period in which it became apparent that the Bolivian economy was suffering from government operation of the petroleum and tin-mining industries, Gulf Oil came into Bolivia under a 1955 petroleum code drafted specifically to encourage the return of foreign companies. Gulf's forty-year lease was only thirteen years old when it was terminated by nationalization. But note again that unlike IPC in Peru, BOGOC was able to negotiate an equitable compensation agreement which was apparently acceptable to both sides. Thus, however arbitrary and questionable Bolivia's actions were, the government has proved willing to pay the price of national pride and independence. To the extent that is true, the nationalization of BOGOC becomes just another chapter in the approach-avoidance quandary in which so many Latin American and other Third World countries find themselves when faced with foreign control of a key asset.

I. BOLIVIA: NEGOTIATING A SETTLEMENT

If the Bolivian case is remarkable for anything, it is for the fact that nationalization came almost without warning, for BOGOC had begun operations in Bolivia in a new era and had been most accommodating to the governments with which it dealt. On several occasions it had agreed to changes in its terms of operation, to benefit the Bolivian Government at BOGOC's expense.[7] In addition, BOGOC provided loans to finance projects of the Bolivian national oil enterprise (YPFB) in supposed joint ventures with BOGOC. There was of course nationalist resistance to and resentment of BOGOC's influence and presence in Bolivia, but it is difficult to imagine what more the company might have done to allay criticism, at least in its official relations.

Expropriation of BOGOC was quick, total, and probably as painless as such a process can be for the foreign investor. Gulf Oil instigated no legal proceedings against the basic action[8] and made no

[7] *See* Radmann, Nationalization in Bolivia 5–6.

[8] Executive Vice-President Lumpkin indicated BOGOC's "properties were illegally seized." Lumpkin, *supra* note 5, at 472.

Gulf Oil did attempt to stop shipments consigned to BOGOC in Bolivia by bringing proceedings translated in 10 INT'L LEGAL MATERIALS 1–6 (1971).

appeals to the government, nor did it turn to the State Department to intercede on its behalf.[9] It really had no need. As if to demonstrate that the nationalization was strictly politics and that there was no ill will involved, the Bolivian Government maintained amicable contact with Gulf Oil almost constantly from the time it took its property[10] to the time it agreed upon the compensation to be paid for it on September 10, 1970, less than one year after the takeover.[11] The only interruption in negotiations was by Gulf Oil and that apparently elicited a complaining letter from the Bolivian Minister of Mines and Petroleum, Marcello Quiroga, inquiring as to why the oil company did not resume talks.[12] As early as December 28, 1969, Bolivia had contracted the French firm Géopétrole to evaluate the "net unrecovered investment of BOGOC in Bolivia."[13] In fact, the dispatch and efficiency necessary to reach accord on not only compensation for but also the continuing enterprise of all facets of a complex industrial and financial structure must be some indication of the seriousness, dedication, and cooperation of the parties on both sides of the negotiations.

Some measure of how unexpected the expropriation was for BOGOC may be taken from the extent and diversity of its commitment to the oil industry in Bolivia in late 1969. The company was in anything but a defensive stance. It had apparently realized no significant profit of any sort on its Bolivian venture.[14] Instead, it

---

[9] *See* Lumpkin, *supra* note 5, at 477.

Gulf Oil's' Chairman of the Board probably urged the State Department to apply the Hickenlooper Amendment to Bolivia shortly after expropriation, but the matter appears not to have been pressed as subsequent events made it unnecessary. Radmann, Nationalization in Bolivia 26 n.33. The State Department was involved in an attempt to bring the Bolivian Government together with Spanish petroleum interests, who might have participated in the management and international sales from what had been BOGOC's enterprise. That initiative faded before final arrangements were made. *See id.* at 13–17.

[10] This may have been contemplated by the Bolivians from the first, for Article 4 of the nationalization decree created an "indemnification commission." *See* Supreme Decree No. 08956 of Oct. 17, 1969, *translated in* 10 INT'L LEGAL MATERIALS 175 (1971). At any rate, Gulf Oil felt communications were kept up. *See id.* at 173.

Relations between BOGOC and the present Bolivian Government have continued in a cordial vein since the agreement as well. When the natural gas pipeline was officially opened, Gulf Oil officials attended as guests of the government and received an audience with President Banzer. Telephone interview with T. Lumpkin of June 28, 1972.

[11] *See* Supreme Decree No. 09381, 10 INT'L LEGAL MATERIALS at 182 (1971).

[12] *See* Radmann, Nationalization in Bolivia 11.

[13] Preamble to Supreme Decree No. 09381, note 11 *supra*.

[14] *See* Lumpkin, *supra* note 5, at 472; Radmann, Nationalization in Bolivia 4–5.

was still busily engaged in creating the infrastructure for its total operation. BOGOC had loaned YPFB and the Bolivian State several million dollars, sometimes taking set-offs against future taxes in return. In addition to over $103 million it had invested in exploration, drilling, and other costs of field development, BOGOC had spent $24 million building its share of a pipeline to carry crude oil over the Andes to the Pacific coast and loaned $10 million to finance YPFB's share of the same pipeline, which was completed in September 1966. In June 1968 BOGOC, YPFB, and an Argentine state company signed an agreement by which the first two would unite in a joint venture under the name YABOG to pipe natural gas from Santa Cruz to the Argentine border. A $46 million pipeline was needed for which Gulf helped line up financing and had contributed over $11 million by October 1969. At the time of nationalization BOGOC and YPFB had apparently all but agreed on a joint exploration venture in the highlands.[15]

Gulf Oil and Bolivia apparently had no disagreement over the evaluation and accounting that found BOGOC's "net unrecovered investment" to be $101,098,961.11, against which a "sole tax" of 22 percent was to be levied, leaving BOGOC with the right to recover $78,622,171.44 in compensation.[16] The indemnity amount will be paid, without interest, by diverting 25 percent of the export proceeds from all "hydrocarbons" (crude oil and natural gas) from the Caranca, Colpe, and Rio Grande fields into a BOGOC Indemnity Trust Account for which First National City Bank serves as trustee. Payments will continue for twenty years or until the indemnity is paid off, whichever occurs first.

Debts outstanding to the World Bank, Inter-American Development Bank, and the New York State Common Retirement Fund (all of which helped finance the natural gas venture) will be paid out of the remaining 75 percent of the natural gas export proceeds. All these debts will be paid off by 1991, according to the debt amortization schedules included in the trust agreement, which again names First National City Bank as trustee to receive the proceeds and to distribute them among the creditors. Where gas proceeds fall short the difference will be made up by diverting the remaining 75 percent of crude oil proceeds to debt service. Gulf Oil has a final, separate claim for $11,073,101.06 on the basis of a "conciliation of

[15] This list of BOGOC's investments and enterprises is gleaned from Lumpkin's and Radmann's treatments, *id.*, and the official documents and accounts in 10 INT'L LEGAL MATERIALS (1971).

[16] *See* Supreme Decree No. 09381, note 11 *supra,* and the agreements implementing it, 10 INT'L LEGAL MATERIALS 1113–50 (1971).

accounts" with the Bolivian Government. Primarily for loans to YPFB and tax credits, this amount is to be paid out of crude oil proceeds, but it is second to the other debt claims in priority.

Although there are complexities not dealt with here, in broad strokes this is the arrangement negotiated by Gulf Oil with the Bolivian Government. Gulf Oil apparently accepted an arrangement which depends on a strong Bolivian State effort in the management of BOGOC's former enterprise. In light of that fact, Gulf may have been more willing to agree to terms in the final indemnification agreement calling for it to turn over all BOGOC's files relating to Bolivian activity and to ship materials destined for the natural gas pipeline and processing plants but held up after nationalization. Also, the agreement is made conditional upon "normal commercialization of the hydrocarbons destined for export" and approval of a World Bank loan to finish the natural gas pipeline to Argentina, two matters that could prove troublesome to Bolivia if either Gulf Oil or the United States government wished to take reprisals against Bolivia.[17]

The legal documents left in the wake of BOGOC's expropriation are relatively few, and none of them is likely to be very controversial, unless a surge of Bolivian nationalism leads at some future date to a decision to default compensation payments and to disavow the debt, a development which is not entirely out of the question.[18] In comparison to the volumes of documents and secondary sources necessary to understanding the IPC case in Peru, the Bolivian documentation is almost minuscule. What we do have is a nice piece of legal drafting by someone who made a neat package of a convoluted set of circumstances and apparently served both sides well in doing so. When one contemplates the potential sticking points that were successfully negotiated and the various parties that were satisfied, one marvels again at the spirit of accommodation that must have prevailed on all sides, but particularly on the parts of Bolivia and Gulf Oil. The documents we have in the BOGOC nationalization might as well be the legal record of any matter-of-fact corporate takeover of any ongoing enterprise as the resolution of an inter-

---

17 These conditions are set out in Supreme Decree No. 09381, art. 6, 10 INT'L LEGAL MATERIALS at 186–87 (1971).

18 At present the Bolivian administration of President Banzer seems disposed to woo foreign capital, and a key element in effective encouragement will be faithful payment on its Gulf Oil debts. However, Banzer is the second president since Ovando, who ordered the nationalization, and there has been some rumbling against foreign investment, although not against the indemnification agreement with BOGOC.

national controversy. Indeed, the very word *controversy,* so apt for many cases of expropriation, seems ill-fitted to this case. No doubt most of the companies who have weathered or are still engaged in more controversial affairs and have the files to prove it would gladly trade their livelier reading for BOGOC's record. The documentation of success may be simpler than that of frustration.

II. PERU: TAKING WITHOUT COMPENSATION

The nationalization of BOGOC came as a shock not only to the petroleum community, but to the world at large. The action of Peru's Revolutionary Government in taking over La Brea y Pariñas should have surprised few observers. In retrospect, there are two more or less amazing aspects to the case. First, it is incredible that IPC was able to function for forty-six years under a fifty-year special regime established by an international arbitration award which was the target of almost constant criticism from the time of its promulgation in 1922 without any government repudiating the arrangement, *i.e.,* to almost complete a term which was ever a festering sore on the conscience of the country. Second, when termination was effected it escalated into the total collapse of all of IPC's Peruvian enterprise, a concern with preeminent position and a bright future in Peru's oil industry, for which La Brea y Pariñas represented little more than an almost-depleted field, whatever its historical role in the establishment of IPC in Peru.

The nub of the controversy over La Brea y Pariñas was that IPC claimed special rights of private ownership in the subsoil resources, a unique exception to the long-standing Peruvian (and Latin American) doctrine that all mineral wealth belongs to the state and may be exploited only under concession agreement. On several occasions the Peruvian political process took the issue to the brink of repudiation of IPC's special status in the La Brea y Pariñas field. In every instance that special status escaped unscathed, although every such episode may have heightened Peruvian national resentment and frustration with the situation.

Others, including the author, have dealt with the history of the controversy in greater detail. In the interests of brevity—for the story is a long and complex one with tantalizing gaps to conjecture upon—only those aspects of La Brea y Pariñas history which are necessary to the legal aspects of the controversy and its "Peruvian solution" will be treated here. Suffice it to note that when President Fernando Belaúnde Terry took office in 1963, the question was of sufficient magnitude that he made its solution one of his highest priorities and promised to send a law embodying a definitive termination of the problem to Congress within ninety days of assuming the presidency. Belaúnde kept his promise, but an opposition Congress whose majority was not entirely unsympathetic to IPC's interests and pressure by the United States Embassy and State Department prevented immediate settlement and dragged the matter on for five years until August 1968, when Belaúnde was finally able to announce an agreement. Whether because the Peruvian populace, whipped by anti-IPC journalism and the passage of time, had become vindictive and demanding toward IPC and disenchanted with Belaúnde's efforts, or because the agreement was in fact unfair to Peru, which had seemingly come out on the short end of every confrontation over La Brea y Pariñas, the agreement rapidly became the target of strong criticism.

On October 9, 1968, less than one week after it deposed the constitutional regime of President Belaúnde, the Revolutionary Government sent troops to take possession of the La Brea y Pariñas oilfields and the Talara industrial complex held and operated by IPC up to that time. The action was characterized as the initiation of a constitutional expropriation of private property for public purposes, save with respect to the subsoil petroleum deposits, the taking of which was carried out as *revindicación,* or recovery by the rightful owner of property held by another. The more important subsequent developments in the Peru-IPC case proceed directly from the October 9, 1968, actions of the Revolutionary Government and are consequent upon the legal nature of the earlier action.

Perhaps the most important element in the government's case is the *revindicación* of the subsoil petroleum deposit. The essence of the *revindicación* action is that the government claims a right to recuperate the oil reserves as they existed in 1924. For the part of those reserves which was extracted and cannot be replaced, the government asks $690,524,283 as restitution. As a direct consequence of the claim for restitution against it, IPC so far has received no money compensation for its expropriated property. The Peruvian Government recognized its constitutional duty to pay fair value for all of IPC's assets that it expropriated but charged such compensation off against its own claim for restitution. Since its property in Peru never reached $690.5 million by anyone's estimate, IPC conceivably will never receive any compensation for the property it has lost, unless some departure from the restitution claim is allowed.

Throughout its handling of the controversy with IPC the Revolutionary Government has been adamant in two respects: first, that the matter is one controlled exclusively by the internal laws of Peru and, secondly, that the matter is being conducted in strict adherence to those laws. Thus, all remedies open to a private party under Peruvian domestic law are available to IPC insofar as they may apply to the instant circumstances. These propositions will serve as the point of departure for this short investigation. We propose to trace what domestic law has been applied thus far and to demonstrate as completely as possible how IPC has fared at the hands of Peruvian justice and why.

IPC instituted two major appeals against the action of the Revolutionary Government: (1) in the Peruvian courts, attacking the constitutionality of the method of expropriation of IPC's northern installations and the cancellation of an agreement signed by the oil company and government which had been represented as "the complete and definite solution of the matters pending in the La Brea y Pariñas affair," dated August 12, 1968; and (2) in the Ministry of Energy and Mines, an administrative appeal against the declared debt of $690,524,283 for restitution of the La Brea y Pariñas oil deposit of 1924 to the State.

A. The August 1968 Agreement

The settlement negotiated between IPC and Belaúnde's government was in the form of a contract signed by the two parties and registered before a Lima notary on August 14, 1968. Empresa Petrolera Fiscal (the Peruvian state oil company, hereafter EPF) signed two additional contracts with IPC concerning the sale by EPF to IPC of crude oil and natural gas produced in La Brea y Pariñas.

The main contract stipulated that IPC recognized the Peruvian State's eminent domain, renounced all potential claims to the La Brea y Pariñas subsoil, and transferred to the State all IPC rights in the surface, including those installations used in the extracting process. The refinery and related installations were to be retained by IPC, which under the contracts signed with EPF would have purchased up to 80 percent of EPF production of crude oil and all of the natural gas from La Brea y Pariñas. The State also agreed to cancel all money claims it may have had against IPC as a result of its administration of the La Brea y Pariñas field since 1924 and to guarantee IPC's existing and future concessions in other parts of Peru. The parties declared that the agreement had "totally and definitively resolved" all matters pending in the La Brea y Pariñas controversy.[19]

Final resolution of the matter was not so easily achieved, however. The Executive had negotiated the agreement under two laws: Law No. 16674 of 1967, in which Congress had responded to popular pressure by commanding the Chief Executive to take La Brea y Pariñas back for the State, and Law No. 17044 of 1968, a very general delegation of powers for a sixty-day period during which the Executive was empowered by law to "prescribe extraordinary measures to, inter alia, promote the complete development of the economy."[20] In each case of specific Executive action under the delegatory law, Law No. 17044, account was to be rendered to Congress after the fact, so that the legislature could then—consistent with Peruvian practice—debate the measure and, if it desired, exercise a veto.[21] No express approval by Congress was necessary, since Law No. 17044 required none. However, although a "final" agreement had been signed, the Peruvian State arguably was not fully bound until the agreement was approved—either specifically or tacitly—in Congress. In the meantime, the Executive began to implement the terms of the contract through a series of administrative decrees and resolutions.[22]

Amid increasingly critical popular comment on the settlement, Congress had not approved the contract when it adjourned on September 6, 1968. Objections and protests were further heightened when the president of EPF resigned and then went on national television to denounce the crude oil contract as invalid, claiming a crucial eleventh and final page had been signed but deleted from the version ultimately made public.[23] When the military deposed

[19] The main contract is published in 2 CONTROVERSY, Doc. No. 51, and also in 7 INT'L LEGAL MATERIALS 1217 (1968); the crude oil contract in 2 CONTROVERSY, Doc. No. 55, and also in 7 INT'L LEGAL MATERIALS 1231 (1968); the natural gas contract in 2 CONTROVERSY, Doc. No. 57, and 7 INT'L LEGAL MATERIALS 1226 (1968).

[20] Law No. 17044 of June 20, 1968.

[21] *See* Furnish, *The Hierarchy of Peruvian Laws,* 19 AM. J. COMP. L. 91, 95–96 (1971).

[22] *See* 2 CONTROVERSY, Docs. No. 52–57, including S.D. No. 088–68–FO of Aug. 13, 1968; S.R. No. 0020–68–FO/PE, and S.R. No. 0020–68–FO/PE, all of Aug. 14, 1968. *See also* 7 INT'L LEGAL MATERIALS 1226–44 (1968).

[23] Whether in fact the page in question ever existed or, if it did, what may have happened to it, seems impossible to determine with any degree of reliability. Perhaps the most plausible explanation of the famous "missing eleventh page" is that of Goodwin, *supra* note 3, at 80–86, but it does not explain what happened to the page.

Belaúnde on October 3, 1968, in its first official act it promulgated Decree-Law No. 17063, the Statute of the Revolutionary Government. The first article of this brief charter of the de facto administration hinted that one of the primary reasons for its assumption of power was the junta's dissatisfaction with the settlement in the La Brea y Pariñas case.[24] In its substantive provisions, the Statute of the Revolutionary Government established that a junta of the commanding generals of the army, the navy, and the air force should designate a President[25] who would exercise all the functions ascribed to the Chief Executive under the Constitution plus, with the approving vote of his Cabinet, all those powers assigned by the Constitution to the legislature.[26] The Revolutionary Government pledged itself to act in conformity with the Constitution and other laws of the State "insofar as they may be compatible with the objectives of the Revolutionary Government."[27]

B. The Revolutionary Government and IPC

The de facto government turned immediately to the La Brea y Pariñas issue. Decree-Law No. 17065 of October 4, 1968, annulled the settlement contract with IPC and all other acts and obligations of the State undertaken in consideration of it. On October 9, 1968, Decree-Law No. 17066 declared the expropriation of the Talara industrial complex, proceeding on the assumption that *reivindicación* of the subsurface oil deposits had already been initiated. The government invoked the Constitution and Law No. 16674 as the bases for the expropriation, which commenced the same day when troops were sent to Talara to take possession from IPC.

When EPF assumed the administration of the La Brea y Pariñas field and refineries, an ad hoc arrangement was made under which IPC took the production of the field from the refinery and retailed it through the IPC distribution network. The crude production of the contiguous Lima concession, which remained in IPC's possession, also continued to be processed through the Talara refinery.

No wholesale price for the petroleum products was fixed at the

---

[24] "The Armed Forces of Peru, duly . . . conscious of the immediate necessity of putting an end to . . . the surrender of natural resources of wealth . . . as well as to the loss of the principle of sovereignty . . . assume responsibility for the direction of the State, for the purpose of moving it ahead toward the definitive achievement of national objectives."

[25] Decree-Law [hereinafter cited as D.L.] No. 17063, Oct. 4, 1968, art. 4.

[26] *Id.* art. 6.　　　　[27] *Id.* art. 5.

beginning of the period. The parties were supposed to settle their differences by accord shortly thereafter, but when EPF sent IPC an invoice for $11.7 million in petroleum products delivered up to December 31, 1968, IPC protested that payment would mean operating its retail network at a loss and that no special account had been made for crude oil delivered from IPC's Lima concession to the Talara refinery for processing.[28]

The government attempted to freeze IPC's accounts to coerce payment, as had been done successfully earlier on a tax claim,[29] but discovered that IPC had run its Peruvian bank accounts into the red while repatriating $14 million at the favorable certificate rate of exchange between January and October 1968. The repatriations paid back dollar loans from United States banks for IPC equipment purchases, and further repatriations on the same loans were authorized on November 5, 1968, by the Revolutionary Government's Minister of Finance.[30] IPC's exchange operations were unquestionably legal, but the fact that they had been permitted cost a Minister of Finance and several high officials in the Central Reserve Bank their jobs.

Closely following this episode, the Peruvian Government announced on February 6, 1969, that IPC owed it $690,524,283 in restitution for all of the mineral products it had removed from La Brea y Pariñas since May 1924.[31] As security against the $690.5 million and other debts, EPF physically and legally moved in as trustee of all of IPC's Peruvian operation.[32] Following the process to its logical termination, on August 22, 1969, the government moved to expropriate the "totality of [IPC's] economic activities."[33]

C. IPC's HABEAS CORPUS APPEAL

Less than a week after the military government took possession of La Brea y Pariñas and its installations, IPC filed a petition in

[28] *See* 2 CONTROVERSY at 27–30; *Comisión Encargada de Fijar Responsabilidades en Control y Administración de los Bienes de la IPC,* INFORME 20–30 (1969).

[29] *See* S.R. No. 1070–H, Nov. 10, 1967; Official Communique of Ministry of Finance, Nov. 29, 1967, in 1 CONTROVERSY, Doc. No. 31.

[30] These events are detailed in INFORME, *supra* note 28, at 5–19.

[31] Ministerial Resolution [hereinafter cited as M.R.] No. 0017–69–FO/PE, Feb. 5, 1969.

[32] Notice of Preventive Embargo of Feb. 6, 1968, 2 CONTROVERSY, Doc. No. 80.

[33] S.D. No. 014–EM/DGH, Aug. 22, 1969, preamble. However, because of IPC's debit accounts all money and credits in favor of or against IPC were excluded from the expropriation. *See id.*

the Superior Court of Lima, Fifth Correctional Tribunal, attacking the constitutionality of the two decree-laws under which the Revolutionary Government had acted.[34] IPC's petition was submitted as an "appeal of habeas corpus."

Habeas corpus is a very broad remedy in Peru, having evolved beyond the more limited application of the remedy of the same name in the common-law jurisdictions from which it was originally adapted to the Peruvian system. Under the present Peruvian Constitution and laws,[35] habeas corpus has become a general summary action available to any natural or juridical person as a means of impugning any official action that may infringe his "individual and social" constitutional rights.[36] The action is sometimes characterized as an appeal because it is initiated at the first appellate level in the court system and is limited to issues of constitutional law.[37]

IPC's habeas corpus petition specifically attacked the constitutionality of Decree-Laws No. 17065 and No. 17066 and all official acts dependent on them. Against the first decree-law, IPC's major argument was that under article 220 of the Constitution only the judicial branch legitimately could annul the La Brea y Pariñas settlement agreements between IPC and the deposed constitutional regime. Article 220 vests the power of administering justice in the courts, and IPC contended that the military executive had usurped that power by promulgating a law invalidating a contract and other juridical acts in consideration of it. Supporting reference was made to Article 19 ("Those acts are null which usurp public function . . . .") and to Article 228 ("[T]erminated process may not be revived.")

Decree-Law No. 17066, under which the government had taken immediate possession of IPC's surface rights and improvements in La Brea y Pariñas, was impugned as a violation of private property rights guaranteed under: (1) Article 29 provisions against expropriation without prior judicial process and indemnification; (2) the freedom-of-commerce-and-industry clause of Article 40; and (3) the prohibitions against confiscation of private property in Articles 29 and 57.

On the above grounds, IPC asked that the decree-laws in question

[34] Expediente [hereinafter cited as Exp.] No. 161/68, Oct. 14, 1968; English translation in 2 CONTROVERSY, Doc. No. 67.

[35] CONSTITUTION OF PERU art. 69; CODE OF CRIMINAL PROCEDURE arts. 349–59; ORGANIC LAW OF JUDICIAL POWER art. 141 (7).

[36] *See, e.g.,* Bustamante Cisneros, *Constitución y Habeas Corpus,* 18 REVISTA DE JURISPRUDENCIA PERUANA 244 (1960); Cooper, *Habeas Corpus in the Peruvian Legal System,* 30 REVISTA DE DERECHO Y CIENCIAS POLÍTICAS 297 (1967); Ferrero, *Garantías Constitucionales,* 27 DERECHO 35, 36–37 (1969).

[37] *See* Cooper, *supra* note 36, at 328–32.

should be found inapplicable and that the violation of its constitutional rights should be terminated by restoring matters to their status prior to the promulgation of the decree-laws. The habeas corpus was found inadmissible by the Fifth Correctional Tribunal;[38] that ruling was upheld on appeal to the Supreme Court,[39] one judge in five dissenting.

In initiating its habeas corpus action IPC may have been attempting to follow the successful example of another Peruvian oil company, Conchan Chevron. A short time before, on August 3, 1968, Conchan Chevron had received a favorable verdict from the Fourth Correctional Tribunal of Lima in a habeas corpus action against three supreme decrees of the Belaúnde government that attempted to create special privileges for the state oil company, EPF, by discriminating against the operations of Conchan and others holding long-term concessions.[40] Even though it cited one of the same constitutional provisions, IPC's habeas corpus was quite different in substance. The issue in IPC's action was not discrimination. Rather, possession of property, expropriation procedures, and the annulment of an agreement on petroleum rights were at issue, and the official dispositions under attack were decree-laws of a de facto government rather than supreme decrees.

The Fifth Correctional Tribunal, probably affected by the supercharged political atmosphere in which IPC's habeas corpus was heard, handled the case very badly. Its written opinion finding for the validity of the Revolutionary Government's decree-laws is unusually prolix and intemperate for a Peruvian court, making it difficult to extract substantive reasoning from the opinion.[41] The Peruvian Supreme Court, taking the case on appeal, exercised a more judicious touch.

The Supreme Court majority wrote a typically short, unelaborated opinion which did not develop or expose the high court's reasoning. Such substantive discussion as it contains accounts for less than half of a 344-word opinion. The Supreme Court noted that Decree-Laws No. 17065 and No. 17066 had been promulgated "in accordance" with earlier laws of Congress[42] and according to proce-

---

[38] Exp. No. 969/68, R.S. of Nov. 9, 1968 (Trib. Corr., 5a. Sala).

[39] Exp. No. 939/68, R.S. of Jan. 3, 1969 (Corte Suprema, la Sala) (4–1 vote).

[40] Exp. No. 1278/67. R.S. of Aug. 3, 1968 (Trib. Corr., 4a Sala). Conchan Chevron relied primarily on Article 23 (equality of persons before the law) and Article 40 (freedom of commerce) of the Peruvian Constitution.

[41] For a more detailed analysis of the lower court opinion, see Furnish, *supra* note 3, at 362–66.

[42] Specifically, Laws No. 9125 of June 4, 1940; No. 14696 of Nov. 5, 1963; No. 16674 of July 16, 1967; and No. 17044 of June 10, 1968.

dures fixed by the Statute of the Revolutionary Government, Decree-Law No. 17063. Without further elaboration, the decision
stated, "[I]t is not required for the exercise of a right by its natural
owner that a prior judicial declaration should be pronounced concerning it, since its existence, based on a law, is superior and
precedent to any judicial decision and requires none to preserve it
intact."[43]

Taken as a general proposition, the Court's language might express the antithesis of the rule of law, *i.e.*, under this rule any party
could unilaterally impose whatever he considered to be his "natural
rights," secure in the belief that they were "superior and precedent
to any judicial decision." However, Peruvian courts do not operate
on the principle of stare decisis. The *ratio decidendi* in a given case
is not necessarily expected to stand as a precedent or to be consistent with the past cases.[44] Supreme Court opinions often offer
neither a detailed discussion of the sources relied on nor a careful
exposition of the way in which the announced propositions lead
to the result. Thus, the Peruvian high court, even in its most important decisions, writes almost as an oracle, in the sense that its
rulings are apt to be brief and cryptic. Elaborating where the Court
did not may seem to be a fruitless exercise, but it presents the only
possibility of deriving meaning that will fit a vague statement to a
specific result.

IPC's argument that the military government lacked the constitutional power to nullify IPC's August 12, 1968, agreement with the
deposed Executive is based on the supposition that both parties had
completed all the formalities necessary to bind themselves. However, the Executive had acted under a special sixty-day delegation
of powers in Law No. 17044 when it negotiated and accepted the
agreement.[45] Under the law, the Executive was required to "give
account" to Congress of its special actions. Thus, the constitutional
legislature may have had a right—still unexercised at the time of
the military coup—to consider the Executive's "final solution" to
the La Brea y Pariñas problem and reject it.[46] According to its basic
statute and the recognized practice of military governments in Latin

[43] In the original: ". . . el título de un derecho no requiere para su ejercicio
que, previamente, una declaración judicial se pronuncie sobre el, ya que su
existencia, basada en la ley, as superior y anterior a toda decisión judicial por
lo que no requiere dejarlo a salvo." Note that *titular* may also be translated
"title holder" rather than "natural owner" as the author has done here.

[44] *See* Furnish, *supra* note 21, at 101.

[45] As recognized in S.D. No. 080–68–FO, Aug. 9, 1968, authorizing signature of
the contract, and in the contract of Aug. 12, 1968, as well.

[46] *See* Furnish, *supra* note 21, at 96 n.12.

America, the Revolutionary Government has the legislative prerogative, which it exercises through the President and his Cabinet.[47] Arguably, then, Decree-Law No. 17065 did no more than apply the legislative prerogative specifically reserved in Law No. 17044: the right to review and reject Executive action based upon that law.

Other of IPC's constitutional arguments simply appear untenable under the clear terms of the Constitution itself. Recent amendments to Article 29, which provide for compensation in long-term bonds or by other manner of deferred payment "which the law shall establish" where expropriation of sources of energy is involved, would seem to give the government a right to possession prior to compensation.[48] Freedom of commerce and industry, as guaranteed in Article 40 and upheld in the Conchan Chevron habeas corpus case, would appear to be no bar to exercise of the State's right of eminent domain through proper expropriation proceedings.

No such ready explanation exists for the Revolutionary Government's possession of the La Brea y Pariñas field and installations as the first step in an expropriation proceeding. Article 29 of the Constitution states that no one shall be deprived of his property without due process of law, a provision which quite clearly appears to have been violated. Although the seizure was justified in the preamble to Decree-Law No. 17066 "to ensure the administrative collection of IPC's outstanding debts," and although Law No. 16674 authorized the Executive to expropriate La Brea y Pariñas "taking into account . . . IPC's debts to the State," under normal circumstances such dispositions should not mitigate the constitutional prerequisite of judicial process before the State may take possession of property it wishes to expropriate.[49]

Perhaps the Supreme Court's holding is consistent with that part of the Fifth Correctional Tribunal's opinion which can be interpreted to mean that the Revolutionary Government enjoyed a constituent license (a right) to depart from constitutional pro-

[47] *Id.* at 95.   [48] Law No. 15252 of Nov. 18, 1964, art. 1.

[49] The government was probably afraid that if it did not take immediate possession of the industrial complex, it would be left in the hands of a party faced with a large debt and possibly resentful of the government's action, thus not disposed to play the role of faithful trustee of a vital industrial resource. *See* address by García Montúfar, legal adviser to the Ministry of Energy and Mines, Expropriación de Propiedad Extranjera, Protección Diplomática y No Intervención, presented to the Lima Bar Ass'n, Jan. 9, 1969. This is not of course a constitutional justification, but a similar process was employed when large coastal sugar plantations were occupied by government administrators the day after it was announced they would be expropriated, probably for similar reasons. *See* D.L. No. 17716 of June 24, 1969, art. 61.

cedures in its expropriation of the La Brea y Pariñas surface property. Perhaps the Supreme Court's ambiguous opinion goes even further, holding that so long as the Revolutionary Government acts through decree-laws (the right to govern according to its Statute, Decree-Law No. 17063) the Court will not presume to review its action.[50] The latter might be more plausible in the light of Latin American custom and practice with de facto governments.[51] Further, the Peruvian Supreme Court has never held a law of Congress or a decree-law unconstitutional.[52]

A definitive interpretation is made difficult not only because the Supreme Court opinion is vague in its positive aspects but because a negative element is added. It approves only the result of the Fifth Correctional Tribunal, disclaiming "the other matters contained" in its decision as "irrelevant and untenable" (*insubsistente*). Whether this refers to the intemperate and erroneous statements in the lower court's opinion, or to all or portions of its substantive discussion, is unclear. The dissent, as brief and vague as the majority opinion, sheds no light on the matter. In any event, such ruminations hold no comfort for IPC at this juncture, for whether in the Court's mind the Revolutionary Government had an unchecked power to violate the Constitution at will or something short of that, it did annul IPC's settlement agreement and possess its property unchecked by the written constitution or the judicial power.

D. The $690, 524, 283 Debt Claim and IPC's Administrative Appeal

Perhaps the single most important aspect of the La Brea y Pariñas controversy is the $690,524,283 debt the Peruvian Government claims against IPC. It is this debt and the legal basis upon

[50] The Dictamen Fiscal, or recommendation of the Supreme Court's independent counsel, seemed to urge that construction. *See* Exp. 939/68, Dictamen Fiscal, Dec. 13, 1968 (Cte. Sup., 1a Sala).

[51] This would be in keeping with the theory that any successful revolution brings with it a "destruction of the country's constitutional substance, for . . . no pre-revolutionary Constitution can claim validity in such circumstances; the basis of its effectiveness, its *grundnorm*, has perished before a new, superior norm-creating force." Cooper, *supra* note 36, at 306. *See also* Irizarry y Puente, *The Nature and Powers of a "Defacto" Government in Latin America*, 30 Tul. L. Rev. 15 (1955).

[52] *See* Furnish, *supra* note 21, at 97–107.

which it is claimed that make the case unique.[53] Because of the debt, IPC may never collect any compensation for the investments taken from it by the Revolutionary Government: all indemnification for expropriated property will simply be embargoed and charged off against the debt, which surpasses all estimates of IPC's total assets in Peru prior to October, 1968.[54] Finally, most of the more difficult and central questions of law in the case are met over the issue of the debt.

The $690.5 million debt represents restitution for all of the minerals extracted from the La Brea y Pariñas field during the period in which IPC claimed ownership, March 1, 1924, to October 8, 1968.[55] Stated another way, the debt restores to the Peruvian State the value it enjoyed in the La Brea y Pariñas subsoil petroleum deposit on March 1, 1924, which was subsequently lost through IPC's exploitation of the field. Accordingly, the amount of the debt was determined by a relatively simple method: production totals for crude oil, natural gas, and liquified propane gas during the period in question were each multiplied by a standard wholesale unit price minus freight and costs of production.[56]

Legally the debt forms an integral part of the Peruvian State's *reivindicación* of the La Brea y Pariñas subsoil petroleum deposits. *Reivindicación* is a word which has its demagogic uses in Latin America, and it was probably in this popular sense that it was applied to the nationalization in Bolivia. However, it is also a rather precise legal term and was used as such in Peru. According to the classic definition, *reivindicación* refers to the right of an

[53] In addition, the Peruvian Government has declared that IPC owed an amount of "more than $54,848,308.10" for compulsory investments it did not make after 1959 and for harmful production methods employed after relations with the Peruvian Government worsened. Informative Bulletin No. 18 of the Ministry of Energy and Mines, May 13, 1968, in 3 CONTROVERSY, Doc. No. 197.

Although other possible debts have been mentioned, and even reported, the Peruvian Government's specific claims have never exceeded the following: (1) $690.5 million for restitution of La Brea y Pariñas petroleum deposits, (2) $54.8 million for obligatory investments avoided, and (3) $9.2 million for products delivered by EPF to IPC between October 9, 1968, and January 20, 1969. This treatment concentrates on the first debt, as the parties have.

[54] *See* D.L. No. 17517 of March 21, 1969.

[55] M.R. No. 0017–69–FO/PE of Feb. 6, 1969, preamble.

[56] *Id.* appendix, in 2 CONTROVERSY, Doc. No. 79; 8 INT'L LEGAL MATERIALS 300–04 (1969). The prices utilized seem arbitrary; the East Texas price for crude oil is one of the highest in the world and relatively little of the La Brea y Pariñas crude was sold in the United States during IPC's administration. Further, the United States price has increased recently with respect to the international market.

owner not in possession of his property to recover it from a possessor who has no property right in it.[57] The Peruvian Government, claiming the right of *reivindicación* in the name of the State, takes the position that "juridically the real property constituted by a mine is the deposit of substances in solid, liquid or gaseous state . . . a property which, by its peculiar nature, disappears to the extent that it is the object of exploitation or use."[58] Thus, consistent with the concept of *reivindicación* and the special depleting nature of petroleum deposits, the State not only may claim direct possession of the mineral resources remaining in the La Brea y Pariñas subsoil but also may require restitution for the part that has been removed. Good faith of the putative possessor is no defense to the obligation to make restitution where depletion of the property has occurred. *Reivindicación* involves no question of the use by the possessor; it simply forces him to surrender all of the property to the owner, making reparation for whatever part of the original property cannot be returned. Other adjustments between owner and possessor are necessary, but the essence of the action of *reivindicación* is the recuperation by the owner of his original property.

1. The Procedure

The IPC was not notified of the $690.5 million debt until February 6, 1969, almost four months after the Revolutionary Government forcefully occupied La Brea y Pariñas. Computation of the debt and official notification were made by the Ministry of Development and Public Works, which was instructed by Decree-Law No. 17066 to "commence and carry out the process of expropriation" of the surface and installations of IPC's La Brea y Pariñas property, taking into account "for the purposes of compensation, the amount of IPC's debts to the State, whose collection will be effected." Coincidentally with the notification to IPC of the $690.5 million claim against it, a "preventive embargo in the form of

---

[57] *See, e.g.,* Cabanellas, 3 DICCIONARIO DE DERECHO USUAL 527 (1954). Replevin was a similar action at common law.

The Peruvian Civil Code does not include a lengthy provision for *reivindicación* as, for example, the Chilean Civil Code does. *Compare* PERUVIAN CODE, art. 850, *with* CHILEAN CODE, arts. 889–915. Nonetheless, the institution is well known. In the IPC case the *reivindicación* would probably have been an ad hoc remedy since neither the Civil Code nor any other existing statute with provision for *reivindicación* would have applied to the case.

[58] S.R. No. 0095–69–EM of Aug. 6, 1969, preamble.

intervention" was placed on all its remaining assets in Peru.[59] In effect, the government took over IPC's total operation, under a procedure for the "coactive" collection of public debts established by Decree-Law No. 17355 of December 31, 1968.

As before, IPC was quick to attack the government's action. Within two weeks the company filed an administrative appeal against the ministerial resolution fixing the debt.[60] Unsuccessful in the Ministry of Development and Public Works,[61] where the resolution originated, IPC renewed its appeal to the highest administrative level, the President of the Republic, where it was also rejected.[62] The restrictions on public debtors created by Decree-Law No. 17355 gave IPC no other means of attacking the debt; all judicial recourse was blocked until the entire claim was paid to the Peruvian State.[63]

2. IPC's Allegations

In essential part, IPC's petition before the Ministry of Development and Public Works stated:

[We] have no debt whatever to the State for the value of the products which we have extracted from La Brea y Pariñas from 1924 to October 9, 1968, inasmuch as such extraction was done on the basis of our title as owners of said oilfield . . . . [A]ssuming that our title as owners of the La Brea y Pariñas oilfields should not be recognized, it would still be impossible to doubt our good faith possession . . . . Moreover, we point out that in the period of more than forty years in which we have been possessors of the La Brea y Pariñas oilfields, such possession has been public, peaceful, consented to by several governments . . . and has never been judicially questioned.[64]

[59] *Notice of Preventive Embargo*, 2 CONTROVERSY, Doc. No. 80; 8 INT'L LEGAL MATERIALS 305 (1969).

[60] IPC appeal of Feb. 21, 1969, in 2 CONTROVERSY, Doc. No. 81; 8 INT'L LEGAL MATERIALS 316 (1969).

[61] M.R. No. 144–EM/AT of July 8, 1969.

[62] S.R. No. 095–EM of Aug. 6, 1969.

[63] IPC's appeal was under S.D. No. 006–SC of Nov. 11, 1957. Although the Organic Law of Judicial Power, D.L. No. 14605 of July 23, 1963, art. 10, would allow a court to take an issue from the Executive branch whenever a "litigious question" is involved, the Revolutionary Government's more recent Regulation to the General Norms of Administrative Procedures, D.L. No. 17355 of Dec. 31, 1968, art. 6, leaves it to the discretion of the agency whether to suspend the administrative process and allow interlocutory recourse to the judiciary.

[64] IPC appeal of April 22, 1969, against M.R. No. 0017–69–FO/PE, in 3 CONTROVERSY, Doc. No. 93.

In its brief and unembellished allegations, IPC tacitly presumed that the La Brea y Pariñas controversy was controlled by the provisions of the Peruvian Civil Code. If this were true, the case would have been a simple one under the normal rules of Peruvian real property law and IPC's legal position would have been remarkably strong.[65] However, since long before the founding of the Peruvian Republic, mineral resources have been subject to a regime of special obligations and limitations which forms an autonomous legal system, exclusive of the Civil Code. Fundamental to this special system is the classification of mineral resources as a part of the public domain of the Peruvian State, a type of property outside the private-law system established by the Civil Code and other statutes.

The fact that public, and not private, law is primarily involved does not foreclose all possibility of applying Civil Code provisions to actions involving petroleum resources or to IPC's specific case; in case of lacunae in the special laws, recourse is to the general principles of law and equity, to the common law expressed in the Civil Code and other general laws.[66] Thus, there are several crucial threshold issues to be resolved. First, given that a special legal regime does exist for petroleum deposits, what are its rules and how should they apply in the La Brea y Pariñas case? Are there lacunae in the special regime that should have been filled by recourse to the general sources of law? Second, are there facts and law that might have created an exception and thrust the La Brea y Pariñas subsoil petroleum deposits outside the purview of the special legal regime and back into the general?

3. The Administrative Decision and IPC's Title Claim

The Ministry of Development and Public Works rejected IPC's appeal without discussion of the substantive issues. However, on the presidential level denial was handed down in an extensive opinion which represents the first definitive official declaration of the Peruvian Government's legal position in the case.

The Executive flatly denied the possibility of a private title to the subsoil of La Brea y Pariñas, stating that petroleum deposits may be exploited only under concessions formally awarded by the State, regardless of whatever facts and / or law a private party might argue

[65] *See e.g.*, CIVIL CODE arts. 818, 834, 871, 1052.

[66] *See* M. ALZAMORA VALDEZ, INTRODUCCIÓN A LA CIENCIA DEL DERECHO 267 (1964).

as an exception.[67] Normally, an enterprise should not care whether
it has absolute title to mineral resources. Title to a depleting asset
is ultimately no more valuable than a simple concession, provided
that the exploiter plans to exhaust the minerals in question and
taxes are not a factor. However, in the La Brea y Pariñas case IPC
enjoyed a special tax regime at least in part because of the claim
that it and its predecessors made to absolute title rights in the subsoil. IPC was not willing to abandon that claim so long as its special
tax regime was less onerous than that available under a common
concession.[68] In addition, IPC's title claim represented the only
justification outside of equity for its presence as exploiter of the
field for forty-four years. No specific concession was ever granted for
petroleum operations in La Brea y Pariñas. The Arbitration Award
of 1922, which created the unique arrangement under which IPC
operated there, was annulled by Law No. 14696 in 1963, and while
jurists may debate the validity of that unilateral action academ-
ically,[69] the Award is almost certainly void *ab initio* before the
Peruvian courts, since the Supreme Court recognized Law No. 14696
as one of the bases for rejecting IPC's habeas corpus.[70]

Peruvian commentators support the Executive's categorical rejection of even the possibility of absolute private title to subsoil
petroleum. They contend that the eminent domain of the state over
petroleum and other mineral resources creates a special status for
such property within the "public domain," inherent (*inmanente*)
to the State and inalienable.[71] They cite earlier cases of mines that

[67] S.R. No. 095–EM of Aug. 6, 1969, in 3 CONTROVERSY, Doc. No. 109.

[68] *See* Petition of IPC to the Director of Petroleum, Aug. 8, 1957; S.R. of
Nov. 18, 1957 (rejecting petition).

[69] Two distinguished Brazilian jurists, Valladâo and Carneiro, have dealt
with the problem in terms favorable to IPC. *See* their essays in A. OSORES,
M. VILLARAN, H. VALLADÂO, L. CARNEIRO & L. ECHECOPAR, LA BREA Y PARIÑAS:
DISCURSOS ANTE EL SENADO Y DICTAMENES JURÍDICOS 57, 67 (1963).

On the other side, see Castañeda, *supra* note 3, at 5. In 1960, a commission
including such Peruvians as Víctor Andrés Belaúnde (once President of the
U.N. General Assembly), José Luis Bustamante y Rivero (ex-President of Peru
and of the International Court of Justice), and Alberto Ulloa (San Marcos
University professor and author of a much-heralded treatise on Public International Law) found that "[t]he 1922 agreements are essentially defective
[*viciados en su esencia*], but what cannot be ignored is that they have created
a status that has been in effect for 38 years, and a unilateral decision on points
which might have been subject to international decision . . . would be undesirable."

[70] *See* Exp. 939/68, S.R. of Jan. 3, 1969 (Cte. Sup., 1a Sala).

[71] Properties of the State are divided by most treatises into three classes:
public use (roads, parks, rivers); *public benefit* (mines and concessions); and
private use of the State (offices, vehicles, furnishings). The most problematical

were "sold" to private parties by the Crown but on judicial review
were pronounced no more than perpetual concessions. "Owners"
continued to pay all taxes and respect all obligations of the concessionaire.[72] This construction is derived from a long and un-
varying series of laws which provided that mineral resources are
the State's property and may be exploited only under express governmental authorization and payment of the proper tax (*canon*).
In Spanish legislation, this rule may date from the year 1128 and
the promulgation of the *Fuero Viejo de Castilla;* most colonial
legislation clearly reserved title to minerals to the Crown.[73] Curi-
ously, the law was probably the same under the Incas, before Pi-
zarro arrived in Peru.[74] It has been the rule of all the mining codes
enacted by the Peruvian Republic and has been included in the
country's petroleum codes since their inception in 1873.[75] Peru has
never had a general law which recognized private parties' rights
to more than a concession in subsoil petroleum resources.

Peru is not alone in its legal stand against private title to minerals. There is unanimity throughout those Latin American nations
in which mineral wealth plays an important role in the economy.[76]
Although at one time three of the countries—Mexico,[77] Colombia,[78]

---

classification is that of public benefit, which may involve elements of both the
others. However, in the La Brea y Pariñas case it is essential that the minerals
in question fall into the public domain, for private use property of the State is
probably subject to all the rules governing rights between private individuals,
i.e., the Civil Code.

  The chief exponent of the Peruvian argument placing the mine in the public
domain is Castañeda, *Propiedad,* note 3 *supra.* Zárate Polo might not go quite
so far in his *Impugnación a la Tesis de la International Petroleum Co. sobre
la Propiedad Absoluta que se Atribuye, del Subsuelo y de los Yacimientos
Petrolíferos de "La Brea y Pariñas,"* 18 REVISTA DE JURISPRUDENCIA PERUANA
458, 482 (1960). Most of the following legislative history is from Castañeda's
article, verified by the author's research. *But see* A. OSORES, M. VILLARAN,
H. VALLADÂO, L. CARNEIRO & L. ECHECOPAR, LA BREA Y PARIÑAS: DISCURSOS ANTE
EL SENADO (LEGISLATURA EXTRAORDINARIA DE 1917) 5 (1963). An excellent source
book is A. VELARDE, HISTORIA DEL DERECHO DE MINERÍA HISPANO-AMERICANO
(1919).

[72] *See* Zárate Polo, *supra* note 71, at 459; Castañeda, *Propiedad* 12.

[73] *See especially* NOVÍSIMA RECOPILACIÓN, LIBRO IX, TÍTULO XVIII, LEY 1;
ORDENANZAS DE MINERÍA DE NUEVA ESPAÑA, TÍTULO V arts. 1–2; TÍTULO VI art.
1, INC. 22; Castañeda, *Propiedad* 6–9.

[74] Castañeda, *Propiedad* 13 and authority cited therein.

[75] These were the codes of April 28, 1873 and Jan. 12, 1877, the MINING CODE
of 1901, and Petroleum Law No. 11780 of March 12, 1952.

[76] *See, e.g.,* DOMINIO Y JURISDICCIÓN DEL SUBSUELO, PRIMERA PARTE (R. Diaz ed.
1960) including three studies of the question.

[77] Law of June 4, 1892, arts. 4–5; Law of Nov. 22, 1884, art. 10, IV.

[78] Law No. 30 of Oct. 22, 1903, art. 3; Law No. 38 of 1887, Ch. I. art I (3).

and Brazil[79]—permitted the owner of the surface automatic and complete title to the subsoil rights as well, all have since abolished that possibility.

Against the imposing legislative tradition to which the commentators point, IPC raises two exceptions that it contends should have given it title to the La Brea y Pariñas subsoil: (1) a specific transfer of absolute title by the government in 1826 under an explicit law in derogation of the general scheme and (2) prescriptive acquisition, through long and uninterrupted exercise of all title rights.

In 1825, following its successful fight for independence, the new Peruvian Republic found itself in debt to many of its supporters. Simón Bolívar, as acting Chief Executive, signed a law providing that "all class of properties, [including] mines, . . . which belong to the State, and which may be freely disposed of, should be applied to the extinction of the public debt."[80] Under this law and its subsequent regulations, the State discharged its 4,964 peso debt to Don José Antonio de Quintana by giving him title to "the pitch mine, at Prieto Hill in the Department of Piura, known as Amotape."[81] The official act of transfer declared that the State's authorized agents

> desist, quit, and part from the State which they represent, the action, property, and domain it has in the pitch mine referred to . . . and they cede, renounce, and sell it to the buyer or whomever he represents, so that having the title in the form in which they authorize it to him, he may dispose of it freely in the manner most convenient to him. . . .[82]

IPC traced the first of its claims to the La Brea y Pariñas subsoil petroleum principally from the language of that nineteenth-century transaction.

To this observer, IPC's title claim could not prosper on the strength of what the young Peruvian Government ceded to its creditor, Quintana, almost a century and a half ago. The Peruvian commentators' argument that any transfer of absolute title would be null *ipso jure* is persuasive.[83] But even if the State could have

---

[79] Decree No. 4265, Jan. 15, 1921, art. 5.   [80] Law of March 5, 1825.

[81] Registry of Sale, Sept. 28, 1826, in Lima Registry; S.D. of Sept. 22, 1826. In the latter, the department cited is La Libertad rather than Piura, but clearly Piura is correct. The mistake probably resulted from the fact that Quintana was from Trujillo, in La Libertad.

[82] Auto of Sept. 30, 1826.

[83] *See* Zárate Polo, *supra* note 71, at 460. Zárate argues that the 1825 law permitted the State to sell only those mines "of which it could freely dispose" and the regulations to the law, issued on Nov. 8, 1825, clearly specify (arts. 1 and 4) "caved-in, water-filled, or abandoned mines" and no others.

delivered a valid title giving Quintana and his successors absolute rights in subsoil petroleum, the facts and the law indicate it probably did not do so. Whatever passed in title to Quintana in 1826, it seems doubtful that it was absolute soil rights general enough to include petroleum deposits lying under a surface area of over 410,000 acres, the expanse of the present La Brea y Pariñas hacienda.

IPC's advocates have argued that the expansive and general right may be inferred from the history of pitch-mining operations in the area. In the colonial period, private parties renting from the Spanish Crown worked the pitch flows that occurred at several points scattered over a surface area probably even greater than that held by IPC. The operations were carried out by individuals who gained a monopoly over the entire area in return for the annual rent payment. These extensive operations were often referred to generally as the Amotape Mines, although the rental agreements also included more specific boundary descriptions.[84] IPC contends that since the act of transfer to Quintana simply described the property as the "Amotape Mine" located at "Prieto Hill," with no statement of bounds, it must be interpreted to conform to the extensive "Amotape Mine" described in the prior monopoly rental agreements. Support for this position may also be found in the fact that Quintana and the owners who followed him apparently interpreted the title in that way and the commercial operation apparently continued for many years, over the same territory covered by the Crown monopoly.[85] The Peruvian Government never protested the pitch-mining operation.

However, the colonial rent agreements contain other facts that may bear on the 1826 transfer. They cite "Prieto Hill" as a landmark establishing a single side of the area in question.[86] Further, as early as 1775, Don Agustín de Ugarte paid 2,500 pesos a year to the Crown for a pitch-collecting monopoly. In 1802, Don Juan Cristobal de la Cruz agreed to pay 6,000 pesos a year for the Amotape monopoly and the pitch mines of Santa Elena in Guayaquil, farther to the north. Apparently, the rent was assigned equally to each concession, or 3,000 pesos a year for Amotape.[87] In 1825, preparatory to the title transfer, the State valued the mine it gave to Quintana

---

[84] *See* LONDON & PACIFIC PETROLEUM CO., HISTORIA DE LA BREA Y PARIÑAS art. V (2d ed. 1960); 3 CONTROVERSY, appendix to Doc. No. 110; L. ECHECOPAR GARCÍA, RATIFICACIÓN DE MI INFORME JURÍDICO SOBRE EL CASO DE LA BREA Y PARIÑAS 21–24 (1960).

[85] *See* L. ECHECOPAR, *supra* note 84, at 23.

[86] *See* 3 CONTROVERSY, Appendix to Doc. No. 110.   [87] *Id.*

at 2,695 pesos, although the latter accepted it in total payment of the debt of 4,964 pesos.[88] In the meantime, the Constitution of 1823 had abolished the Crown monopolies, so that it would not have been unnatural to sell a piece of what had always been a unitary operation.[89] As pointed out above, pitch mining was still apparently a thoroughly viable commercial enterprise, and it is doubtful that an operation over so extensive an area as IPC claims could have declined so drastically in value between 1775 and 1825.

Even if IPC were able to establish that the Quintana title was valid as an exception to the norm that private parties could never take more than a concession to mineral resources and that it covered all the surface area of the present La Brea y Pariñas hacienda, it would have had to show that the "pitch mine" transferred in 1826 included not merely pitch, which appeared at the surface, but the liquid and gaseous hydrocarbons in the subsoil below. The point may be debatable,[90] but the Peruvian legislative tradition against alienation of the State's domain in mineral resources would seem to command a strict interpretation and presumptions that run against IPC.

The special property status created for mineral resources by the same strong legislative tradition described above was essential to the denial of IPC's other claims. Once petroleum resources are classified as part of the public domain of the State, falling within the ambit of public (instead of private) law,[91] it follows logically and properly that no prescriptive acquisition may run against the State's title to the property,[92] that the State's claim is not even prescribed by administrative acts such as those issued in 1887 and 1888, and that administrative (not judicial) process will be used for many of the relevant decisions. This simple fact, so essential to

[88] *See* S.D. Sept. 22, 1826.   [89] Constitution of Nov. 12, 1823, art. 155.

[90] *Compare* L. ECHECOPAR, *supra* note 84, at 13–21 (1960), *with* Zárate, *supra* note 71, at 461–62.

[91] The public law—private law distinction, which may never concern the common lawyer, is ingrained in the civilian from the time of his first exposure to legal education and continues throughout his professional career. It is a basic and important distinction within the civil-law traditions from which Peru draws its legal system.

The dichotomy is often drawn on the basis of civil and commercial law on the private law side and constitutional and administrative law on the public law side. Another general way of distinguishing the two is to say that public law deals with relations in which the State is involved and private law controls relations between private individuals.

[92] *See* CIVIL CODE arts. 822 (4), 823; PETROLEUM CODE, Law No. 11780 of 1952, art. 1. These more recent provisions recognize a rule extant since colonial days, as authoritatively traced in Castañeda, *Propiedad*.

the civil-law traditions that make up Peru's legal system, contained the basic answer to most of the issues raised by IPC in its administrative appeal.

Much of IPC's difficulty throughout the administrative process and other official proceedings stemmed from its attempt to apply private-law concepts and norms, *i.e.*, the provisions of the Civil Code relating to property rights between private individuals, to what are public-law issues or matters covered by special legislation. For this reason, much of the law IPC cited in support of its positions was inapposite, no matter how the rule might have favored IPC if it could have been applied. In the mass of petitions and pleadings it submitted to the executive and judicial powers, IPC never fully developed the threshold question of why private-law, rather than public-law, rules should control the controversy. However, despite the fact that most of the applicable laws favor the government position, they do not independently resolve the case. La Brea y Pariñas was and is a unique question in Peruvian law, which cannot be resolved satisfactorily without recourse to considerations outside the written norms.

In its treatment of IPC's administrative appeal the Supreme Resolution of the Executive most closely resembled a brief for the government position, especially on several of the minor points.[93] It would be difficult to characterize it as an objective consideration of the facts and law involved. The Supreme Resolution did not consider any potential equities on IPC's side of the case. Still, in any equitable treatment of the facts, IPC should have strong arguments in its favor. For forty-four years it operated the La Brea y Pariñas fields in substantially the same manner as any concessionaire, paying those taxes required of it by the State and complying with most of the other substantial obligations pertaining to petroleum concessions, albeit favored by a special arrangement reducing its tax burden as set out in the Arbitration Award of 1922. Even accepting the fact that tacit concessions do not exist, it would seem that long practice and use should have made some sort of equitable consideration of the La Brea y Pariñas question necessary to a creditable solution to the problem. *Reivindicación* itself is an ad hoc action as

[93] For example, the Executive finds an admission by IPC against interest, in a clause of the August 12, 1968, Agreement IPC signed with the Belaúnde regime which exonerates the company from all debts it "may have owed the Government." In a similar vein, the Supreme Resolution finds all laws and decree-laws in question are valid because Article 132 of the Constitution provides that laws take effect the day after their official publication. *See* S.R. No. 095–EM of Aug. 6, 1969.

applied to La Brea y Pariñas;[94] thus an equitable balancing of interest and contributions would appear to have been desirable. What the final result of a review in equity might be is probably beyond the capacity of anyone's conjecture. It is doubtful that a simple solution exists; *e.g.*, putting IPC in the position of a common concessionaire in 1924 and simply charging the difference in taxes actually paid and taxes that would have been paid under normal legislation since then.[95]

It is almost certain that IPC will be given no equitable hearing in the foreseeable future. In its own way the La Brea y Pariñas case is just as purely political as the expropriation of BOGOC in Bolivia. But while the latter might be likened to a simple skit on the stage of Latin American foreign investment, seeming (though perhaps not to Gulf Oil) hastily contrived and quickly terminated, La Brea y Pariñas seems more a ponderous epic presentation, defying comprehension and analysis. The story of petroleum in Peru begins with it, and the eras of foreign investment may be measured against it: from promoters scrambling to bring in a venture in a new industry to diplomatic intervention by commercial powers to corporate arrogance and privilege to, most recently, the good corporate citizen.

The whole set of circumstances must be set in political perspective to be fully understood. One should not underestimate the intense public feeling, built up over the years by the journalism of *El Comercio* and other influential Lima newspapers and magazines, that La Brea y Pariñas represented an old injustice perpetrated against the Peruvian nation, a score which had to be settled. When IPC's La Brea y Pariñas operation is viewed in the light of Peruvian popular opinion as the shameful and irritating vestige of another era in foreign investment in that country, harsh treatment of the oil company becomes more understandable, if no easier to justify.

Under Standard Oil ownership IPC was at least ostensibly a model corporate citizen, but IPC paid not for its own sins so much as for those of all its predecessors and the Peruvian governments

---

[94] There is some analogy for it in the present MINING CODE of 1950, art. 67, which provides for reivindicación between private concessionaires. The MINING CODE of 1901 contained the same provision in Article 112. *See also* note 57 *supra*. However, some authorities would argue that the State exercises a "right of sovereignty through administrative processes" instead of proper *reivindicación*. *See* F. VIDELA ESCALA, EL DOMINIO DEL ESTADO SOBRE LAS MINAS 46–47 (1965) and authority cited therein. The substantive effect is the same.

[95] *See* note 53 *supra*, plus the multifarious claims introduced in the legislative bills before Congress in 1960. *See also* the relevant study by E. ELEJALDE *et al.*, note 3 *supra*.

with which they worked. The delay in taking definitive action during the first five years of the Belaúnde regime, at a time when public attention was continually focused on the issue, almost unquestionably increased the minimum conditions acceptable to the Peruvian populace. Thus, if the $690.5 million debt appears blown out of all equitable proportion as applied to a company which apparently relied, in good faith, throughout forty-four years on an arbitration award which lacked only four years of expiring, its dogmatic expression—based as it is on substantial legal foundations—may be most comprehensible as simply a tenable justification for Peru's total takeover of IPC's going enterprise. Whether Peru will bargain down from that figure at some future date is impossible to predict, but under the legal theory invoked any reduction in IPC's debt would be a clear concession.

Peru and the Revolutionary Government have been more responsible throughout the La Brea y Pariñas controversy than many casual observers may realize. Legal procedures were followed throughout the affair, if not always with total equanimity. There is a solid basis in law for all that Peru has done. If Peru has been less than equitable in applying the full force of its law to divest an oil company of its whole operation, one might objectively balance this against the fact that the ultimate confrontation took place on legal grounds that the company chose not to abandon gracefully and graciously (albeit at a high cost) when it might have had the chance.

III. CONCLUSION

For two cases that occurred so close to each other in geographical and temporal terms, and that manifest such outward similarity, the BOGOC and IPC cases were in fact quite different. For the reasons outlined above, the La Brea y Pariñas controversy represents a case unique in petroleum law. It probably generated more legal commentary and writing (wholly leaving aside political treatments) than any other single case in Peruvian history. Most of the issues were well defined and fully developed at least fifteen years ago.

Whatever other observations may be made, it seems indisputable that La Brea y Pariñas is an extremely complex legal controversy. No isolated or clear-cut legal rules control the case; rather it involves some of the most basic and far-reaching questions in the Peruvian legal system. Still, IPC's advocacy throughout many years of difficult procedures has been on the whole extremely complete and painstaking. IPC has made an exceptional public record of the case in all its legal aspects. The Peruvian Executive and Judiciary have accorded IPC full hearing and ample responses on most issues in the case. However, no comprehensive judicial consideration of the equities has been granted, and the governmental action may at times have seemed—especially to the North American lawyer —abrupt or arbitrary in denying what other countries might consider ordinary due process safeguards.

Perhaps this author, out of ignorance, does not assign the BOGOC expropriation the importance that is its due. It is difficult to see it as more than a relatively quick decision to gamble for political gain, perhaps influenced by the effect of the IPC expropriation in Peru as a solidifying factor for a new military regime. If it is unique for anything, it may be for the relatively smooth way in which a settlement was reached. Despite this, however, the BOGOC affair may make it extremely hard for Bolivia to entice another foreign oil company into that country of mercurial political swings on anything but a short-run basis. Peru, on the other hand, appears to have succeeded in convincing several large foreign petroleum concerns that her atmosphere is conducive to doing business in spite of what happened to IPC.

CHAPTER V

An Analysis of the Expropriation
of the Properties
of Sociedad Minera El Teniente
by Chile in
the Light of International Law Principles

PREFACE

ON JULY 16, 1971, the business and properties of the large copper mining industry of Chile (previously owned and operated by three Chilean companies each with mixed United States private and Chilean government ownership) became fully owned by the Chilean State. The expropriation was accomplished by an amendment to the Chilean Constitution approved by both Houses of the Chilean Legislature and signed into law by President Salvador Allende Gossens of Chile. The amendment, together with related transitory provisions, provides for the payment by Chile of compensation in respect of the assets of the expropriated joint mining companies exclusive of the mineral bodies to which they have mining rights and exclusive of certain other properties. Compensation is to be measured by the "book value" of eligible assets at December 31, 1970, less "excess profits" deemed to have been realized since 1955 and less certain other deductions. Any compensation found to be owing by Chile may be paid in installments over not longer than 30 years with interest at not less than three percent.

One of the companies affected by the Chilean Constitutional Amendment is Sociedad Minera El Teniente, S.A. ("El Teniente") which was organized in Chile in 1966. In return for all of its stock, El Teniente acquired in 1967 all of the assets of a wholly owned subsidiary of Kennecott Copper Corporation, Braden Copper Company ("Braden"), a Maine corporation. Fifty-one percent of the stock in El Teniente held by Braden was acquired in 1967 by

This chapter is taken from "Expropriation of El Teniente, the World's Largest Underground Copper Mine," a booklet prepared by Kennecott Copper Corporation in August 1971. The Preface was written by Pierce N. McCreary, General Counsel of Kennecott, and the remaining portion constitutes a Memorandum of August 16, 1971, prepared at the request of Kennecott by its Washington, D.C., counsel, Covington & Burling. Footnotes in the Memorandum have been revised to conform to the style used in this book.

the Corporacion del Cobre ("Codelco"), with the remaining 49 percent being retained by Braden.

On July 16, 1971, all of the assets of El Teniente passed to the Chilean State and the corporate entity known as El Teniente was nationalized, all pursuant to the express provisions of the amendment to the Chilean Constitution. The next day, July 17, an Administrative Commission took physical possession of the assets of El Teniente pursuant to Presidential Decree No. 73 and, in the opinion of our Chilean counsel, Enrique Evans de la Cuadra and David Stitchkin Branover, El Teniente has ceased to exist as a juridical entity.

MEMORANDUM

I. INTRODUCTION

Under generally accepted principles of international law as recognized by the United States and other nations, the taking of the property of an alien for a public purpose is lawful only if there are reasonable provisions for determination and payment of "just compensation," which means that such compensation must be prompt, adequate and effective. Compensation is not prompt, adequate or effective unless the foreign owner of an expropriated business interest receives an amount which is equal to the going concern value of that interest or, at the very least, the full and fair market value of the net assets which are represented by that interest.

In view of these principles of international law, it is necessary to consider the business and properties of El Teniente, the value of the same and how relevant provisions of the recently-passed Chilean legislation would have to be interpreted and applied in respect of the taking of Braden's interest in El Teniente to achieve a result consistent with these accepted international law principles.

II. GOVERNING PRINCIPLES OF INTERNATIONAL LAW

A. Under Generally Accepted Principles of International Law as Recognized by the United States and Other Nations, a Taking of Property of an Alien for a Public Purpose Is Lawful Only if There Are Reasonable Provisions for the Determination and Payment of Just Compensation

1. Decisions of International Tribunals

In its judgment in the *Factory at Chorzow* (*Merits*) case,[1] the
Permanent Court of International Justice recognized that to render
an expropriation of an alien's property lawful a government must
pay "fair compensation" or the "just price of what was expropriated."

Numerous international arbitral decisions have specifically held
that just compensation must be paid by states which expropriate
alien property, notwithstanding that the takings were for a valid
public purpose and in good faith.

For example, in *Melczer Mining Co.* (*United States v. Mexico*),[2]
the United States espoused the claim of a mining company whose
pipe line was seized by the Mexican State of Sonora. Writing for
the Mixed Claims Commission created by Mexico and the United
States in 1924, Commissioner Nielsen stated that "[i]t is unnecessary
to cite legal authority in support of the statement that an alien is
entitled to compensation for confiscated property."[3]

This same principle of international law was recognized in a
decision by the General Claims Commission created by the United
States and Panama in 1926. In the *De Sabla* case,[4] the United States
espoused the claim of an American citizen some of whose land,
Bernardino in the Province of Panama, had been seized by private
persons holding grants of title and licenses to cultivate issued by
the government of Panama. Rejecting various technical defenses
raised by the Panamanian government, the Commission concluded
"that the . . . licenses granted by the authorities on Bernardino
constituted wrongful acts for which the government of Panama is
responsible internationally. It is axiomatic that acts of a government in depriving an alien of his property without compensation
impose international responsibility."[5] The Commission recognized
that the Panamanian government had acted in good faith and
without discrimination and that the government "was endeavoring
throughout this period to bring order out of a chaotic system of
public land administration." Nevertheless, the Commission stated
that "[i]t is no extreme measure to hold . . . that if the process of
working out the system results in the loss of the private property of
aliens, such loss should be compensated."[6]

Finally, Commissioner Bainbridge writing for the Mixed Claims

---

[1] [1928] P.C.I.J., ser. A, No. 17, at 46–47.   [2] 4 U.N.R.I.A.A. 481 (1929).
[3] *Id.* at 485.   [4] (United States v. Panama), 6 U.N.R.I.A.A. 358 (1933).
[5] *Id.*, at 366.   [6] *Id.*

Commission established by the United States and Venezuela held that "[t]he right of the State, under the stress of necessity, to appropriate private property for public use is unquestioned, but always with the corresponding obligation to make just compensation to the owner thereof."[7]

2. Action of Expropriating Governments

Not only have international arbitral tribunals held that there is a duty to pay just compensation for expropriated property, but expropriating governments themselves have recognized this international legal responsibility and submitted to arbitration the amount of compensation due. As early as 1889, in the *Delagoa Bay* case,[8] the Portuguese government which had cancelled a concession for a railroad and seized the enterprise acknowledged its duty to pay compensation and agreed to submit the issue of the amount of compensation due to an arbitral tribunal.

Governments have specifically acknowledged their duty to provide just compensation in their expropriatory legislation. For example, in 1967 the Tanzanian government nationalized nine commercial banks, eight import-export firms and seven milling firms with associated food manufacturing interests. This Tanzanian action was the "first comprehensive program of nationalization to be undertaken in East Africa . . . ."[9] According to the commentator on the Tanzanian action, the legislation, implementing the nationalization provided for "full and fair compensation."[10] The

[7] Upton Case (United States v. Venezuela), 9 U.N.R.I.A.A. 234, 236 (1903). *See also* Hatton Case (United States v. Mexico), 4 U.N.R.I.A.A. 329 (1928). "It is unnecessary to cite legal authority in support of the statement that an alien in the situation of the claimant [whose seven horses were seized by the Mexican federal troops] is entitled under international law to compensation for requisitioned property."

[8] Delagoa Bay R.R. Case (United States and Great Britain v. Portugal), 2 J. MOORE, INTERNATIONAL ARBITRATIONS 1866 (1900), *discussed in* Fachiri, *Expropriation and International Law*, 6 BRIT. Y.B. INT'L L. 159, 165 (1925). For similar examples of cases involving a state's acknowledgment of the duty to pay just compensation for expropriated properties, *see also* Affaire des Proprietes Religieuses (Great Britain, France and Spain v. Portugal), 1 U.N.R.I.A.A. 7 (1920); Norwegian Shipowners' Claims (Norway v. United States), 1 *id.* 307 (1922); British Claims in the Spanish Zone of Morocco, 2 *id.* 615 (1925); and Portuguese-German Arbitration of June 30, 1930, 2 *id.* 1035 (1930).

[9] Note, *Tanzanian Nationalizations: 1967–1970*, 4 CORNELL INT'L L. J. 59, 60 (1970).

[10] *Id.* at 66.

Cuban government also committed itself to this principle in its 1960 legislation implementing its nationalization program.[11] Domke explains that the Eastern European and other communist countries, their declarations to the contrary notwithstanding, have in practice recognized the obligation to pay compensation for nationalized property in negotiated agreements with other communist and with Western countries,[12] while Drucker points out that "Communist states vis-à-vis each other recognize that their . . . measures of dispossession give rise to legal obligations towards those who have been dispossessed."[13]

3. Position of the United States Government

The United States has consistently maintained that under generally accepted principles of international law an expropriating state must provide "just compensation" or "full and fair compensation," which, as demonstrated in Section B of this chapter, means in the case of a business interest, prompt, adequate and effective compensation based on the value of the expropriated interest as a going concern, taking into account the fair market value of all of the assets taken. Although there are earlier examples setting forth the United States position, the classic statement of this principle of international law was made by Secretary of State Cordell Hull in a note sent on July 21, 1938, to the Mexican Ambassador in Washington:

The taking of property without compensation is not expropriation. It is confiscation. It is no less confiscation because there may be an expressed intent to pay at some time in the future.

If it were permissible for a government to take the private property of the citizens of other countries and pay for it as and when, in the judgment of that government, its economic circumstances and its local legislation may perhaps permit, the safeguards which the constitutions of most countries and established international law have sought to provide would be illusory. Governments would be free to take property far beyond their ability or willingness to pay, and the owners thereof would be without recourse. We cannot question the right of a foreign government to treat

[11] Article 24 of the Fundamental Law of Cuba (J.A. 15a, 16a) ; arts. 4 and 5 of Law No. 851 (J.A. 46a, 47a) ; para. 5 of Executive Power Resolution No. 2 (J.A. 69a, 70a) .

[12] Domke, *Foreign Nationalizations, Some Aspects of Contemporary International Law*, 55 AM. J. INT'L L. 585, 603 (1961) .

[13] Drucker, *On Compensation Treaties Between Communist States*, 229 L. TIMES 279, 293 (1960) .

its own nationals in this fashion if it so desires. This is a matter of domestic concern. But we cannot admit that a foreign government may take
the property of American nationals in disregard of the rule of compensation under international law. Nor can we admit that any government unilaterally and through its municipal legislation can, as in this instant case,
nullify this universally accepted principle of international law, based as it
is on reason, equity and justice.[14]

In a further note dated August 22, 1938, Secretary of State Hull
reiterated the United States position in the following terms:

> The government of the United States merely adverts to a self-evident fact
> when it notes that the applicable precedents and recognized authorities on
> international law support its declaration that, under every rule of law
> and equity, no government is entitled to expropriate private property, for
> whatever purpose, without provision for prompt, adequate, and effective
> payment therefor. In addition, clauses appearing in the constitutions of
> almost all nations today, and in particular in the constitutions of the
> American republics, embody the principle of just compensation. These, in
> themselves, are declaratory of the like principle in the law of nations.
> The universal acceptance of this rule of the law of nations, which, in
> truth, is merely a statement of common justice and fair-dealing, does not
> in the view of this Government admit of any divergence of opinion.[15]

The United States has on numerous occasions reasserted the requirement under international law for an expropriating state to
provide prompt, adequate and effective compensation. A number of
examples of the United States declarations in support of this principle and a further defense of the continuing validity of the rule
appeared in a speech delivered in 1961 by the then United States
Legal Adviser, Loftus E. Becker.[16] During that speech Mr. Becker
said: "It is, I think we will all agree, the core principle of international law in . . . [the] field [of property protection] that the
property of foreigners may not be taken by the state without the
payment of just compensation."[17]

It should be clear that the United States has applied the standard
of "just compensation" against itself on behalf of foreign nations.
For example, in June, 1941, the United States requisitioned certain
immobilized Danish vessels under legislation approved by the
Congress. Under the legislation the United States was required to
pay "just compensation" for any property requisitioned.

[14] 3 G. HACKWORTH, DIGEST OF INTERNATIONAL LAW 656 (1942).
[15] *Id.* at 658–59.
[16] Becker, *Just Compensation in Expropriation Cases: Decline and Partial
Recovery*, 53 AM. SOC'Y INT'L L. PROCEEDINGS 336 (1959).
[17] *Id.* at 337.

In a letter to the Administrator of the War Shipping Administration, dated April 16, 1943, Secretary of State Hull stated that he "considered it important that just compensation in the real sense be made to the [former] Danish owners" of the requisitioned ships. In hearings before the House Committee on the Merchant Marine and Fisheries in 1941, Assistant Secretary of State Breckenridge Long stated that "just compensation" would be interpreted by the United States as "heretofore determined by both municipal and international tribunals."[18]

4. Action By the United Nations General Assembly

Finally, the action of the United Nations General Assembly in approving Resolution 1803 (XVII) on "Permanent Sovereignty Over Natural Resources" in 1962[19] confirms that generally accepted principles of international law require payment of prompt, adequate and effective compensation for an alien owner's expropriated property. Paragraph 4 thereof states:

In . . . cases [of nationalization or expropriation] the owner shall be paid appropriate compensation, in accordance with the rules in force in the State taking such measures in the exercise of its sovereignty and in accordance with international law.[20]

We do not presume to say whether the compensation to be paid the former owners of property expropriated under the Chilean legislation is *appropriate* "in accordance with the rules in force in the State [*i.e.* Chile] taking such measures in the exercise of its sovereignty." The question is whether the compensation is *appropriate* "in accordance with international law." The Soviet Union maintained in an amendment twice rejected that compensation was, in effect, *appropriate* if it was in accordance with the rules in force in the expropriating state. The United States, on the other hand, maintained that compensation is *appropriate* only if it is in accordance with domestic law and meets the international law standard of being "prompt, adequate and effective." No delegation took exception to the statement following the Second Committee vote

[18] HOUSE COMM. ON MERCHANT MARINE AND FISHERIES, COMPILATION OF MATERIAL ON THE DETERMINATION AND PAYMENT OF JUST COMPENSATION FOR VESSELS REQUISITIONED UNDER SECTION 902 OF THE MERCHANT MARINE ACT, 1936, H.R. Doc. No. 20, 78th Cong., 1st Sess. 167–73 (1943).

[19] G.A. Res. 1803, 17 U.N. GAOR Supp. 17 at 15, U.N. Doc. A/5217 (1962).
[20] *Id.*

against the Soviet-sponsored amendment by United States Representative Seymour M. Finger, that his delegation was " 'pleased that this Committee has reaffirmed the traditional international law providing for appropriate—this is to say, prompt, adequate and effective—compensation in case of expropriation and the like.' "[21]

B. Under Generally Accepted Principles of International Law as Recognized by the United States and Other Nations "Just Compensation" Means, in the Case of an Expropriated Business Interest, the Payment of "Prompt, Adequate and Effective Compensation" for the Value of the Expropriated Interest as a Going Concern

1. Decisions of International Tribunals

In its decision in the *Chorzow Factory* case,[22] the Permanent Court of International Justice not only recognized the duty to pay compensation to render an expropriation lawful but took note of the standard of compensation required. The Court said that the owner is entitled "to the value of the undertaking at the moment of dispossession, plus interest to the day of payment." The Court specifically referred to the value of the entire enterprise as such, and not to the "book value" or even the separate-asset market value of its properties. This reference can only mean that the measure of just compensation is the going concern value of the expropriated entity.

Judge Parker, speaking as umpire in the proceedings before the United States–Germany Mixed Claims Commission to establish the amount of American claims against Germany arising out of the First World War, stated that

In all claims based on property taken and not returned to the private owner the measure of damages which will ordinarily be applied is the reasonable market value . . . if it had such market value; if not, then the intrinsic value of the property as of such time and place . . . .[23]

---

[21] *Cited in* Schwebel, *The Story of the U.N.'s Declaration on Permanent Sovereignty over Natural Resources*, 49 A.B.A.J. 463, 466 (1963); Letter from Ambassador Adlai Stevenson concerning the status of G.A. Res. 1803, Dec. 21, 1962, in 57 Am. J. Int'l L. 406–07 (1963).

[22] [1928] P.C.I.J., ser. A, No. 17.

[23] Administrative Decision No. III of December 11, 1923 (United States v. Germany), Mixed Claims Commission, [1925–1926] Cons. Ed. of Decs. and Ops. 61, 63.

A specific reference to the going concern value of an entity appears in another opinion by Judge Parker. Announcing the method to be followed by the Mixed Claims Commission in determining the reasonable market value of plants and other properties, Judge Parker said:

In computing the reasonable market value of plants and other properties at the time of their destruction, the nature and value of the business done, their earning capacity based on previous operations, urgency of demand and readiness to produce to meet such demand which may conceivably force the then market value above reproduction costs, even the goodwill of the business, and many other factors, have been taken into account.[24]

In *Norwegian Shipowners' Claims, (Norway v. United States)*,[25] it was said that the standard for compensation required to be paid for property taken by a foreign government is "not only . . . the fair actual value of the property taken, but also . . . at the time and place it was taken . . . and in view of all the surrounding circumstances . . . ."[26]

The principle of requiring the payment of "going concern" value for an expropriated enterprise was explicitly reaffirmed in 1948 by the American Mexican Claims Commission in the *Wells Fargo & Company* case.[27] The claimant owned a one-half interest in a Mexican company operating a railway express business under a franchise from the government-owned corporation, National Railways of Mexico, which owned the other half interest in the express company. After seizure of the company's assets in 1914, the Mexican Constitutionalists issued a decree taking over the railroads and all related services, including the claimant's express business. The Mexican government operated the express business until 1926 when it was turned back to the National Railways.

Wells Fargo filed a claim for its share of net profits from the express business from the date of the expropriatory decree to 1926. In an initial ruling on the Wells Fargo claim Commissioner Under-

[24] Opinion of May 25, 1925 (United States v. Germany), Mixed Claims Commission, *id.* 273, at 331.

[25] 1 U.N.R.I.A.A. 307 (1922).

[26] *Id.* at 334. The United States applies the same standard to its own takings under the fifth amendment of the U.S. Constitution. *See* testimony of Assistant Secretary of State Breckenridge Long in 1941 before the House Committee on the Merchant Marine and Fisheries discussing the Norwegian Shipowners' Claims case and the Supreme Court's decision in Brooks-Scanlan Corporation v. United States, 265 U.S. 106 (1924), note 18 *supra*.

[27] AMERICAN MEXICAN CLAIMS COMMISSION, REPORT TO THE SECRETARY OF STATE 150 (1948), 8 M. WHITEMAN, DIGEST OF INTERNATIONAL LAW 1138 (1967).

wood found that "[t]he measure of recovery should be, not the expected profits over the period of the franchise, but the fair and reasonable value of the property taken augmented by the existence of those elements which constitute a going concern."[28] In addition to making an award for the fair market value of the express company's property taken by the Mexican government, the Commissioner made a separate determination of the going concern value of the expropriated Mexican express company and awarded one-half of that amount to Wells Fargo for its interest in the company.

The claimant appealed the Commissioner's ruling on the ground that the award for going concern value of an expropriated enterprise did not conform to the claim for Wells Fargo's share of net profits in 1926. The full Commission affirmed Commissioner Underwood's initial ruling and quoted with approval the Commissioner's Memorandum referring to the use of going concern value in determining the Mexican "obligation to compensate" for the expropriated enterprise.

2. Restatement of Foreign Relations Law of the United States

In 1964–1965 the American Law Institute published the Restatement (Second) of Foreign Relations Law of the United States.[29] According to the Reporters, the Restatement "in stating rules of international law, represents the opinion of the American Law Institute as to the rules that an international tribunal would apply if charged with deciding a controversy in accordance with international law."[30]

The Restatement provides in Section 186 that the "[f]ailure of a state to pay just compensation for taking the property of an alien is wrongful under international law regardless of whether the taking itself was wrongful under international law."[31] Section 187 defines "just compensation" for purposes of Sections 185 and 186 as being "adequate in amount, . . . paid with reasonable promptness, . . . and . . . paid in a form that is effectively realizable by the alien to the fullest extent that the circumstances permit . . . ."[32]

Section 188 (1) provides that for compensation to be adequate in amount it "must be in an amount that is reasonable under the

---

[28] Commissioner's Memorandum Opinion at 26, *quoted in* REPORT, *supra* note 27, at 152, 8 M. WHITEMAN, *supra* note 27, at 1139.

[29] RESTATEMENT (SECOND) OF FOREIGN RELATIONS LAW OF THE UNITED STATES (1965).

[30] *Id.* at xii.   [31] *Id.* § 186.   [32] *Id.* § 187.

circumstances as measured by the international standard of justice . . . ."[33] This provision goes on to indicate that under

ordinary conditions . . . the amount must be equivalent to the full value of the property taken together with interest to the date of payment

(a) if the property was acquired or brought into the jurisdiction of the state by the alien for use in a business enterprise that the alien was specifically authorized to establish or acquire by a concession, contract, license, or other authorization of the state, or that the alien established or acquired in reasonable reliance on conduct of the state designed to encourage investment by aliens in the economy of the state, [or]

(b) if the property is an operating enterprise that is taken for operation by the state as a going concern . . . .[34]

The official Comment to Section 188 (1) discusses the meaning of "full value" as used in that provision and states that the term means "fair market value if ascertainable." The Comment also provides that if fair market value is not ascertainable, "full value" means the "fair value as reasonably determined in the light of the international standard of justice . . . ."[35] In explaining this concept, the Comment includes the following:

So far as practicable, full value must be determined as of the time of taking, unaffected by the taking, by other related takings, or by conduct attributable to the taking state and having the effect of depressing the value of the property in anticipation of the taking. This does not require, however, disregard of the effect on market values of the state's general power to regulate the use of property or the conduct of business operations.[36]

3. Position of the United States Government

The Reporter's Notes to Section 188 (1) of the Restatement explain that "the United States has taken the unqualified position that international law requires the payment of full value of property taken."[37] An example of what this standard means for the United States in the case of expropriation of an operating enterprise appears in a Memorandum dated November 19, 1962, by the Assistant Legal Adviser for Economic Affairs John B. Rehm:

In the case of an operating enterprise, adequate compensation is usually considered to be an amount representing the market value or "going concern" value of the enterprise, calculated as if the expropriation or

[33] *Id.* § 188 (1) .   [34] *Id.*   [35] *Id. Comment* to § 188 (1) .
[36] *Id.* Comment to § 188 (1) .   [37] *Id.* Reporter's Notes to § 188 (1) .

other governmental act decreasing the value of the business had not occurred and was not threatened.[38]

An example of the United States refusal to accept an alternative, unrealistic basis for valuations arose in connection with the expropriation by the government of Guatemala of 234,000 acres of land belonging to the United Fruit Company. Guatemala fixed the value of the expropriated properties on the basis of their "tax value." In an aide-memoire handed to the Guatemalan Ambassador to the United States on August 28, 1953, the United States asserted that the determination of the value of the properties "on the basis of the tax value . . . bears not the slightest resemblance to just evaluation."[39]

4. Decisions of International Claims Commissions

One important source of internationally accepted valuation standards is the decisions of the international claims commissions established by countries to determine the amount of compensation due for takings after World War II. In the United States, the Foreign Claims Settlement Commission has had the responsibility for determining the value of claims by United States nationals for expropriations by certain foreign countries. In a decision under the Cuban claims settlement program, the Commission held that where appropriate documentation is provided an award will be made for "values higher than those set forth as book values."[40]

In subsequent decisions, the Foreign Claims Settlement Commission has specifically found that "the valuation most appropriate" is one based on the value of the expropriated enterprise as a going concern.[41] In the *Intercontinental Hotels* case, the Commission stated that its basis for valuation "does not differ from the international level standard that would normally prevail in the evaluation of nationalized property."[42] In the *First National Bank of Boston* decision, the Commission stated that "the nature of the business conducted is such that earnings potential reflected in the market price of the stock is of greater significance than asset value

---

[38] 8 M. WHITEMAN, DIGEST OF INTERNATIONAL LAW 1143 (1967).

[39] 29 DEP'T STATE BULL. 357 (1953).

[40] Claim of Berwind Corp., FCSC, ANN. REP. 28 (1968).

[41] *See, e.g.,* Claim of Intercontinental Hotels Corp., Dec. No. CU-4545 (March 4, 1970); Claim of First National Bank of Boston, FCSC, ANN. REP. 33 (1969); Claim of Colgate-Palmolive Co., Dec. No. CU-4547 (March 4, 1970).

[42] Dec. No. CU-4545 (March 4, 1970).

in the determination of true value of the enterprise . . . . [and] at the time of loss the claimant's six Cuban branches had a value exceeding their book value . . . ."[43] Finally, in the *Colgate-Palmolive* case the Commission found that the proper basis for arriving at "going concern" value was to multiply by 15 the net earnings of the two companies in 1959.[44]

This use by the Foreign Claims Settlement Commission of "going concern" value is consistent with the practice of international claims commissions in France and the United Kingdom. In a recently published book Professor Burns Weston concludes after a comprehensive study of the unpublished decisions of the postwar French international claims commissions that these commissions "appear generally to have striven for a distribution based on the 'net market' or 'going concern' value extant ordinarily at the time of loss."[45] Professor Weston adds that when "market quotations have been known, as in the case of many stockholder claims, usually these quotations (or, in their absence, 'nominal values') have sufficed."[46] This study of the French practice indicates that when market quotations were not available the French commissions relied on a number of factors, including "reconstruction costs," annual reports and other indices of the value of enterprises as going concerns.

The postwar British Foreign Compensation Commission adopted a similar "going concern" standard of valuation.[47] According to Professor Lillich, the British Commission followed the general practice in making awards for expropriated property of first determining the net income generated by the property, then establishing the estimated rate of interest from the capital invested in the property and finally calculating the present value of the property using a multiplier based on the interest rate.[48] In valuing expropriated shares the Commission relied on market quotations when available. If such quotations were not available, the Commission utilized balance sheet figures but frequently rendered awards substantially in excess of the nominal value of the shares. Again, it appears that the British Commission, like its United States and French counterparts, took account of the value of these expropriated enterprises as going concerns.

These international and domestic precedents establish the firm

---

[43] FCSC, ANN. REP. 33 (1969).   [44] Dec. No. CU-4547 (March 4, 1970).
[45] B. WESTON, INTERNATIONAL CLAIMS: POSTWAR FRENCH PRACTICE 181 (1971).
[46] *Id.*
[47] R. LILLICH, INTERNATIONAL CLAIMS: POSTWAR BRITISH PRACTICE 112 (1967).
[48] *Id.* at 114–15.

basis for the rule of international law that "just compensation" for an expropriated business enterprise means "prompt, adequate and effective" compensation for the value of the expropriated enterprise as a going concern. There is a specific precedent for determining the value of an expropriated mining enterprise on a going concern basis.

5. Lena Goldfields, Ltd. Arbitral Award

In 1925 the English company, Lena Goldfields, Ltd. was granted a concession by the Soviet government for exploring, mining and transporting mainly iron, copper, lead, zinc, silver and gold. In 1929 the Soviet Union adopted its first Five-Year Plan and began to harass companies such as Lena Goldfields, Ltd., which were considered unacceptable in a socialist economy. Finally, the English company was forced by virtue of a series of Soviet actions in violation of the outstanding concession agreement to cease operations in the U.S.S.R.

The arbitration clause in the concession agreement was invoked by Lena Goldfields, Ltd. When the Soviet Union refused to appear before the tribunal after making an initial appearance, the arbitrators proceeded to decide the case on the basis of the facts available and the submissions of the U.S.S.R. in telegrams explaining that government's refusal to participate in the proceedings. Without any difficulty the tribunal found that the Soviet Union had breached the English company's concession agreement. The tribunal decided that the measure of damages was the "fair purchase price [for Lena Goldfields, Ltd.] as a going concern."[49] In determining the fair purchase price the tribunal utilized a formula which establishes the "going concern" value of the expropriated enterprise by computing "the present value of all of the future profits to be derived from the mine."[50] Under this formula the tribunal determined the estimated annual profit of the various mines held by Lena Goldfields, Ltd., in the Soviet Union. These figures were raised by a "multiplier" which reflected both a rate of interest on the miner's investment and a rate of interest at which the capital invested would be redeemed.[51]

[49] Lena Goldfields v. Russia [1929–1930] Ann. Dig. 3 (No. 1) (Special Arbitral Tribunal).

[50] R. Lewis & Clark, Elements of Mining 359–69 (1964).

[51] *See* unpublished text of Lena Goldfields, Ltd., award at 24–32. *See also* Nussbaum, *The Arbitration Between the Lena Goldfields, Ltd., and the Soviet Government,* 36 Cornell L.Q. 31 (1950).

6. Action of Expropriating Governments

Even those nations which have not expressly recognized the obligation to pay going concern value as such have recognized the obligation to approach this standard by providing compensation equal to the full and fair market value for all of the assets of an expropriated enterprise.

A recent example is in connection with the comprehensive expropriation undertaken by the Tanzanian government in 1967 as part of the Tanzanian plan to create a socialist economic system. The Tanzanian nationalization legislation provided that there would be "full and fair compensation" for expropriated property. Except in the case of companies registered in Tanzania whose shares were acquired, compensation was required for the "net value of the assets taken over."[52]

Among the examples given by Mr. Dias of compensation paid by the Tanzanian government is the agreement with The General Bank of the Netherlands where payment was made for "profits earned but not remitted [by the Bank] before nationalization" and for "the 'true' value of real property [of the Bank] over previous balance sheet valuation."[53] Thus, even a developing country seeking to establish a socialist system of government has agreed to pay for the full and fair market value of the assets expropriated from privately-owned enterprises.

C. Even Where the Expropriation Extends Only to
Selected Assets Under Generally Accepted Principles of
International Law as Recognized by the United States
and Other Nations, "Just Compensation" Means
Payments of Full and Fair Market Value for Those Assets

The form of the expropriation in the Chilean legislation is the taking of all of the assets of the large copper mining companies (Gran Mineria) . However, the purpose and effect of the legislation, as we shall see, is clearly to vest ownership in Chile of the going concern value of the enterprises whose assets are taken. In short, the Chilean legislation is, in substance, although not in form, a taking of the enterprises as operating businesses for which international

[52] Note, *supra* note 9, at 66, *quoting* the 1967 Tanzanian legislation, 6 Int'l Legal Materials 1196–1228 (1967) .
[53] *Id.* at 68.

law requires the payment of compensation for their going concern value.

States have sometimes expropriated selected assets of enterprises rather than all, or nearly all, of the assets comprising the going concern. Unlike the proposed Chilean legislation, these actions involve, both in form and in substance, the taking of less than the going concern value of an enterprise. In these circumstances, generally accepted principles of international law require that the expropriating country pay the alien owner of such enterprises whose assets are taken prompt, adequate and effective compensation equal to the full and fair market value of such assets.

1. Valuation of Individually Expropriated Assets

An early example of this requirement is found in the award by the arbitrators considering the claim of *Henry Savage*.[54] The case concerned the effect of the seizure in 1852 by the government of El Salvador of gunpowder lawfully imported by the claimant. The government decreed that the sale of gunpowder in El Salvador had to be removed before the effective date of the decree or be declared contraband. This governmental action destroyed the market for Savage's gunpowder. The government would not buy Savage's gunpowder except "at prices far below the market value and below the price fixed in the decree."[55]

The United States agreed to espouse Savage's claim against El Salvador for, in effect, expropriating Savage's gunpowder by destroying the market for it. The dispute was referred by the United States and El Salvador to arbitration in Guatemala. In rendering an award for Savage, the arbitrators rejected the El Salvadorian contention that the gunpowder should be valued at prices below market value and below the government-established monopoly price. Instead, an award was made based on either the market value of the gunpowder as alleged by Savage or the government's monopoly price. For another early statement of the standard of compensation required to be paid for expropriated property, see the dispatch by Lord Palmerston in 1846 concerning the Greek government's obligation to provide "full and fair value" for land seized from George Finlay, a British subject.[56]

A classic statement of the meaning of "just compensation" ap-

[54] 2 M. WHITEMAN, DAMAGES IN INTERNATIONAL LAW 894 (1937).
[55] *Id.*   [56] *Id.* at 1386.

pears in the award in the *Norwegian Shipowners' Claims (Norway
v. U.S.A.)* .[57] In that case Norway sought compensation for certain
Norwegian nationals whose ships under construction in the United
States and the contracts therefor were seized by the United States
Shipping Board Emergency Fleet Corporation at the beginning of
World War I. In its award the arbitral tribunal concluded that
regardless of whether the United States seizure was lawful or not
"just compensation is due to the claimants" under both United
States and international law. The tribunal stated that "it is com-
mon ground that such compensation is measured not only by:

    (a) the fair actual value of the property taken, but also
    (b) at the time and place it was taken, and
    (c) in view of all the surrounding circumstances . . . ."[58]

The tribunal added that just compensation "implies a complete
restitution of the *status quo ante*" and is equal to "the real market
value" of the property seized.[59]

2. Arbitral Awards Involving Latin American Countries

A number of the decisions of the American Mexican Claims
Commission demonstrate conclusively that the "just compensation"
to which the owner of expropriated property is entitled is the full
and fair market value for that property at the time of the taking.
The care which that claims commission took in determining the
full and fair market value of expropriated property is revealed in
two decisions concerning land expropriated by the Mexican government. In the first case, claimant sought compensation for a
large tract of longleaf yellow pine timber land expropriated by the
Mexican government. When the American Commissioner made an
award which the claimant considered too low, the claimant appealed relying on the testimony before the Commissioner of "two
disinterested witnesses" who were experts in timber land values
and who "gave evidence as to value" of the expropriated land. The
Commission found that the American Commissioner had given too
little weight to the evidence of the land appraisal experts. It also
held that the price paid for the land by the claimant is "a factor
worthy of consideration although, of course, not controlling." Based
on the available appraisals, the Commission held that the land was
worth two and a half times what the American Commissioner had
awarded.[60]

In the second case, the Commission reviewed a finding concerning

[57] 1 U.N.R.I.A.A. 307 (1922) .   [58] *Id.* at 334.   [59] *Id.* at 338.
[60] Pine King Land and Lumber Co. Case, REPORT, *supra* note 27, at 413.

the value of certain farm land expropriated by the Mexican government in Baja California, Mexico. The land in question had been improved with an irrigation system, which the Commission found justified placing a "high value" on the land but for which the Commission refused to allow an award separate from that for the land. In reaching its determination the Commission took account of the value of each of the improvements on the land and specifically stated that "the *cost* of improvements is not the proper valuation to be placed on the property. It is not the cost but the *value* after construction that determines the value of the irrigation system."[61]

The American Mexican Claims Commission decisions discussed above follow a well-established jurisprudence that "just compensation" for expropriated property means "full and fair market value" at the time of taking. For example, in the *De Sabla* case,[62] the General Claims Commission established by the United States and Panama carefully reviewed various past appraisals and offers for the land, Bernardino, which the Panamanian government had effectively expropriated and made an award based on "as close an approximation to the true value per acre . . . as can be reached."[63] Similarly, in the *Upton* case[64] the United States–Venezuela Mixed Claims Commission allowed compensation for "whatever loss or damage" the claimant had sustained and based its determination on the evidence presented concerning the usefulness of the seized duplicate steel hull.[65]

The United States, of course, is not alone in asserting that the taking of property by a foreign government requires the payment of compensation equal to the full and fair market value of such property. For example, Lord McNair, in a symposium on the Indonesian expropriations of 1958, cites examples of the governments of a number of countries reaffirming that international law requires that such compensation be paid for expropriated property.[66] In that same symposium, Professor Verdross, relying on the *Norwegian Shipowners' Claims* case and other international legal precedents, concludes that an expropriating state has a duty to pay the former owner of expropriated property compensation equal to the amount needed to replace that property in the current market.[67]

[61] Ross Elmer Neel Case, REPORT, *supra* note 27, at 416.

[62] 6 U.N.R.I.A.A. 358 (1933).   [63] *Id.* at 368.

[64] 9 U.N.R.I.A.A. 234 (1903).   [65] *Id* at 236.

[66] McNair, *The Seizure of Property and Enterprises in Indonesia*, 6 NEDERLANDS TIJDSCHRIFT VOOR INTERNATIONAAL RECHT 218 (1959).

[67] Verdross, *Die Nationalisierung niederländischer Untnehmungen in Indonesien im Lichte des Völkerrechts*, 6 NEDERLANDS TIJDSCHRIFT VOOR INTERNATIONAL RECHT 278, 286–87 (1959).

D. Under Generally Accepted Principles of International Law as Recognized by the United States and Other Nations, the Payment of an Expropriation Compensation Award Must Be in a Form and at a Time so as to Represent the Full Value of the Award

To satisfy the requirements of international law, not only must an expropriation award be just, but it must be paid in such a form and at such a time that the foreign party in fact receives the full value of that award. Thus, if payment by the expropriating state is to be made in bonds or other evidences of indebtedness, the obligation issued to the former owner by the state must have a market value when issued equal to the required compensation award.[68]

The United States has referred on a number of occasions to this requirement under international law for full payment of value due for expropriated enterprises and property. For example, following World War II, the government of Rumania enacted legislation authorizing the nationalization of industrial, banking, insurance, mining, transportation and other enterprises. Chapter 4 of the Rumanian law apparently dealt with the payment of compensation to be provided for the expropriated enterprises. Commenting on this Chapter of the Rumanian law, the United States said in a note to Rumania that:

the United States government feels that compensation in the form of bonds of the fund of nationalized industry, redeemable, apparently, from the prospective profits of the individual nationalized enterprises can not be considered to provide prompt, adequate and effective compensation.[69]

In the dispute previously referred to involving the Guatemalan government's expropriation of land belonging to the United Fruit Company, the Guatemalan government offered to pay United Fruit in the form of government-issued 3 per cent "agrarian bonds" maturing in 24 years. The United States stated in its aide-memoire to the Guatemalan Ambassador that:

Payment in bonds maturing in 25 years, with interest at 3 per cent per annum, and of uncertain market value is scarcely to be regarded as either prompt or effective payment. Many of the holders will realize little on the bonds in the course of their lives.

The offer of payment in bonds under all the circumstances is not of a

---

[68] Restatement, *supra* note 29, §§ 187, 188 (especially Illustration 1).
[69] 19 Dep't State Bull. 408 (1948).

nature to offer "the full guarantee and protection" of either Guatemala or of the law of nations.[70]

III. VALUATION OF BRADEN'S INTEREST IN EL TENIENTE IN ACCORDANCE WITH INTERNATIONAL LAW AND UNDER THE CHILEAN EXPROPRIATION LEGISLATION

A. Braden's Present Circumstances and How It Came to This Position

Prior to 1967 Braden was the 100 per cent owner of the El Teniente copper mine and appurtenances which are located approximately 55 miles south of Santiago, Chile. In the early 1960's Braden had completed technical studies for expanding El Teniente's capacity which had reached about 180,000 short tons of copper annually by 1967. The expansion program called for investment of an additional $200 million in the El Teniente mine.

At the time these expansion plans were under consideration, Braden was paying Chilean taxes of between 81 and 87 per cent of its gross income, including a 13 per cent supplemental tax which had been enacted after the 1960 Chilean earthquake. This supplemental tax was progressively repealed for all Chilean taxpayers except Braden and one other large copper mining company. Braden conditioned its undertaking the proposed expansion program on obtaining from the Chilean government a "more reasonable rate" of taxation and guarantees that the rate would not be changed from year to year.[71] Negotiations by Kennecott with the Chilean government in the early 1960's concerning such fiscal guarantees were not successful.

After the election of President Eduardo Frei in 1964 as Chilean President and after successful negotiations between the new Chilean government and the other affected companies, the Chilean government and Kennecott Copper Corporation agreed on December 3, 1964, to a Memorandum of Understanding concerning Chile's direct participation in the ownership and expansion project for the El Teniente mine. President Frei announced the terms of the agreements with the Gran Mineria, including Braden, in a major address to the Chilean people on December 21, 1964. Included in this ad-

---

[70] 29 *id.* 359 (1953).
[71] W. Friedmann J. Beguin, Joint International Business Ventures in Developing Countries 77, 83 (1971).

dress was a description of the "general outlines of his proposed tax program which was vital to the implementation of the agreements [with the Gran Mineria] . . . ."[72]

On September 16, 1966, pursuant to the Memorandum of Understanding, El Teniente was established and in April, 1967, Braden transferred its Chilean properties to the new company in return for all of the stock of El Teniente. Braden sold 51 per cent of its El Teniente stock in April, 1967, to Codelco, a wholly owned, autonomous agency of the Chilean government. Codelco agreed to pay for this stock in escudos the equivalent of 80 million U.S. dollars. Full payment had been made on this obligation by December 31, 1970. Under Ministry of Finance Decree No. 2,046 (September 16, 1966) Braden was exempted from "all taxes, contributions, duties or charges arising from, caused by, or as a consequence of the transfer of its property, assets and liabilities, rights and obligations" to El Teniente, including the tax on the $27.6 million "gain" representing the difference between the amount paid and the original cost of Braden's 51 per cent interest sold to Codelco.[73]

The Chile-Kennecott plan, in which Codelco, Braden and El Teniente joined, called for expanding El Teniente's productive capacity from 180,000 short tons of copper annually to an estimated 280,000 short tons annually by 1972. This expansion, estimated to require approximately $267 million, was to be financed in part from El Teniente's earnings and the balance from borrowings to be protected by Chilean law, including an investment decree by the Chilean Minister of Economy, Development and Reconstruction, and Chilean governmental guarantees.

The Chilean Ministry of Economy, Development and Reconstruction issued Decree No. 316 on March 1, 1967, which authorized El Teniente to invest $230,241,000 in the El Teniente mine and complementary facilities. This Decree also contained significant guarantees concerning the level of taxation applicable until 1987 to El Teniente and its shareholders. It provided in Article 3 (b) that El Teniente would be guaranteed a "sole and invariable" tax of 20 per cent on net taxable income. El Teniente's shareholders were guaranteed under Article 3 (c) of the Decree a "sole and invariable tax at a fixed rate of 30 per cent on dividends and profits distributed" by El Teniente. Interest on credits which Braden would grant to Codelco for purchase of 51 per cent of the shares of El Teniente and to El Teniente were expressly exempted from taxation by Article 3 (f). The Decree guaranteed that El Teniente and its

[72] *Id.*   [73] *See id.* at 85 n.3.

shareholders would be exempted from "any new tax . . . levied on ordinary or excess profits" and that the shareholders would be "totally exempt from taxes on the undistributed profits due to them." Finally, El Teniente was guaranteed that it would "not be burdened with any new taxes or duties, liens or charges, or with any increase in the existing ones" and that any reduction in applicable fiscal charges would be nondiscriminatory. In addition, the Decree contained important guarantees concerning Chilean foreign exchange regulations.

The Chilean Decree of March 1, 1967, authorizing El Teniente to invest $230 million in earnings and borrowings in the El Teniente mine and complementary installations and granting El Teniente and its shareholders certain fiscal guarantees was issued pursuant to the Chilean law then in force. Moreover, Article 10 of the Chilean Constitution provided in 1967 that an expropriated owner has "the right to compensation" and that the determination of the amount of compensation shall be made by a court of law. Under Article 86 of the Constitution in effect in 1967, an expropriated owner can appeal to the Chilean Supreme Court from any decision by a lower court on the amount of compensation to be tendered.

Acting on the basis of these fiscal guarantees and Chilean constitutional safeguards, Braden agreed on April 28, 1967, to lend $80 million to El Teniente in installments corresponding in time and amount to principal payments by Codelco for shares of El Teniente sold to it by Braden. In addition, Braden agreed to lend back to El Teniente upon receipt an amount equal to all of the interest payable until December 31, 1971, by El Teniente on the basic $80 million loan from Braden. This interest loan amounts to about $12,743,000. Installment repayments of the principal of both the basic and additional interest loan from Braden were scheduled to commence December 31, 1971. Payment of the basic and of the additional interest loan were guaranteed by the government of Chile. At December 31, 1970, Braden had lent to El Teniente the basic $80 million and had lent in addition approximately $10,300,-000 representing all of the interest paid by El Teniente to December 31, 1970, on the basic $80-million loan.

Relying on the fiscal and payment guarantees of the Chilean government, the Chilean constitutional protections and on an exchange of notes between the governments of Chile and the United States which made investments undertaken in Chile and approved by the Chilean government eligible for investment guaranty insurance against expropriation and inconvertibility, the United States Agency for International Development ("A.I.D.") issued Contract of Guaranty No. 5670 insuring the $80-million principal of Braden's basic loan to El Teniente and up to one year's accrued unpaid interest thereon, $4,600,000. Early in 1971 this guaranty obligation passed by law from A.I.D. to the Overseas Private Investment Corporation ("O.P.I.C."), a United States government corporation.

In addition, the United States Export-Import Bank ("Eximbank"), relying similarly on the Chilean protections and guarantees, established by an agreement dated May 4, 1967, a line of credit in El Teniente's favor for $110,016,000, to which Braden's loans to El Teniente were subordinated. This credit was also guaranteed by the government of Chile. As of December 31, 1970, El Teniente had drawn down $76,930,000 of its Eximbank line of credit.

To assist in the financing of its expansion program, El Teniente also obtained a commitment from Codelco in 1967 for a loan of $23,700,000 by Codelco to El Teniente. Codelco agreed also to lend back to El Teniente an amount equal to all the interest payable by El Teniente until December 31, 1971 on that loan. This interest loan amounts to about $3,782,000. As of December 31, 1970, El Teniente was indebted to Codelco in the amount of $36,010,000 including amounts borrowed pursuant to this arrangement.

The loans from Braden, Eximbank and Codelco were designed to provide El Teniente with funds of approximately $230 million. The El Teniente expansion program required an additional $53,000,000 to be completed. It was agreed by Braden, El Teniente and Codelco and understood by the Chilean and United States governments, as well as by A.I.D. and the Eximbank, that these additional funds would be supplied from El Teniente's operations. Therefore, these funds could not be distributed as dividends to the owners of El Teniente.

With the Chilean governmental guarantees given and the loans from Braden, Eximbank and Codelco made, the El Teniente expansion program began on schedule. Production capacity had increased to approximately the targeted 280,000 short ton goal by March 1971.

B. The Real Value of Braden's Interest in El Teniente Consistent with Generally Accepted Principles of International Law

As we have said, it is a generally accepted principle of international law, as recognized by the United States and other nations, that the "just compensation" required to be paid to an alien for expropriated property is the full and fair market value of that property at the time of taking. In the case of an enterprise actively engaged in a profitable business this means the full and fair value of that enterprise as a going concern. For the El Teniente mining enterprise, going concern value means what a willing buyer would pay for the El Teniente corporate entity or for all of the business and properties of the corporation, disregarding any Chilean governmental actions associated or contemporaneous with expropriation and having the effect of depressing El Teniente's value.

Using the internationally-recognized standards for valuing mining property which were followed by the *Lena Goldfields* tribunal, the present value of Braden's 49 percent equity investment in El Teniente, reduced by the 30 per cent Chilean dividend tax, is estimated at $175,884,000, assuming a 15 per cent risk rate, a 4 per cent safe or redemption rate, and a $.24 cost / price spread for copper. This figure is conservative. For example, applying realistic capitalization multiples to the over $20 million dividends, net of Chilean withholding tax, paid annually by El Teniente to Braden in recent years, and considering that higher preferential dividends were required to be paid to Codelco while these dividends were paid, that Braden's dividends were reduced by withholding taxes, and also that El Teniente was required to conserve substantial funds for expansion during these years, the going concern value for El Teniente based on earnings would be something on the order of $1 billion ($490,000,000 for Braden's 49 per cent interest). Even this figure does not take into account the increased profitability of El Teniente based upon the 1967–1972 expansion program, which although substantially accomplished by early 1971, had not been reflected in actual production increases through 1970.

As of December 31, 1970, the net worth of El Teniente shown on its books was $328,981,000. Braden's 49 per cent interest in that net worth was $161,200,690. After adding back the $33,419,000 in El Teniente dividends which were declared but have not received the necessary shareholder approval to become a debt of El Teniente, the net worth of El Teniente would be increased to $362,400,000 and Braden's 49 per cent interest therein would be equal to $177,-576,000. This is approximately the same figure derived by applying the customary valuation tests for mineral properties as going concerns described in the preceding paragraph.

The book figures of El Teniente were corrected in 1965 to reflect the true value of its properties as established by a comprehensive independent appraisal made in anticipation of the sale of a 51 per cent interest to Codelco in 1967. That appraisal, by The American

Appraisal Company, established that the fair value of the net tangible assets held by Braden, excluding the value of the ore in and rights to the El Teniente mine itself and construction in progress, were not accurately reflected upon the books of El Teniente at that time. On the basis of this appraisal, the assets sold by Braden to El Teniente have been carried on the books of El Teniente since 1967 at their true values (but not adjusted to reflect the intervening decreasing purchasing power of the dollar). This correction was known to and approved by Chilean government authorities.

The price at which Braden sold a 51 per cent interest in El Teniente to Codelco in 1967 understates the full value of that interest. The 1967 transaction involved far more than a simple sale. It also involved important tax concessions by Chile embodied in legislation. It involved a large expansion program supported by external financing, as well as financing by the government of Chile, designed to enhance the value of Braden's retained 49 per cent interest as well as the interest sold to Codelco. It is clear, therefore, that the 51 per cent interest sold by Braden in 1967 was worth far more than the nominal $80-million sales price. It is also clear that the retained 49 per cent interest was worth far more by the end of 1970, than at the time of the 1967 sale.

Thus, under any reasonable application of generally accepted principles of international law Braden should receive a compensation award of not less than $176 million for its present day equity interest in El Teniente.

C. Compensation Payable to Braden Under the Terms of the Chilean Expropriation Legislation

The Chilean expropriation legislation bases compensation upon the "book values" of certain of the joint companies' assets, excluding any recovery for their most important assets, mineral rights. Amounts could thereafter be deducted from the book value for so-called "excess profits," debts determined by the Chilean State not to have been "usefully invested" and amounts payable by Codelco for shares in the joint mining companies under agreements which the expropriation legislation annuls. Finally, the amount of compensation determined to be owing after all of these adjustments and deductions could be paid on a deferred basis over an extended period of time and with interest which could be lower than rates prevailing in the market.

These are not the standards for expropriation compensation

which have gained recognition and acceptance by the United States and other nations. The following subsections of this memorandum consider essential provisions in the legislation which must be revised, interpreted or found inapplicable in order for Chile to make a fair determination of compensation for Braden's interest in El Teniente.

1. Failure to Compensate for Valuable Mineral Rights and Other Assets

The first and greatest exclusion in the expropriation legislation is compensation for valuable mineral rights. Mineral ores realize their inherent value, for the nation as well as for private enterprise, only to the extent they can be and are recovered, often from deep within the earth, refined, transported and marketed. The role of a mining enterprise is to locate ore bodies, sink shafts to them, bring the ore to the surface, refine it and transport the metal to market for sale.

To encourage investment in a mining enterprise, states protect miners who have found an ore body from encroachment on their claims so long as the claim is worked. Whether this right to work is a proprietary right or not, it is nevertheless a right and a valuable right. Indeed, the members of the Senate Commission which considered the expropriation legislation agreed without apparent exception that the right to work mineral deposits is indeed a valuable right of the mining companies. If that right is taken away prior to its lawful expiration and while the claim is being worked, the owner of that right has lost a valuable interest. If that owner is an alien and the taking of the right is for a public purpose, then, as we have seen above, international law requires that the expropriating state pay just compensation for the full and fair market value of that right.

The statutes of El Teniente dated September 16, 1966, provide (Article 4) that El Teniente's "business will be the continuance of the operations of the mining deposits of Braden Copper Company . . . ." The existence of El Teniente was authorized and its statutes were approved by a decree of the Ministry of Finance dated October 1, 1966. These rights were reconfirmed in the Credit Agreement between El Teniente and Eximbank dated May 4, 1967, which recites in its first paragraph: "Whereas El Teniente owns or will own El Teniente copper mine and related facilities . . . ." The Credit Agreement was made and entered into by El Teniente with the knowledge and assent of the government of Chile and El Teniente's performance was expressly guaranteed by Chile contemporaneously with the Agreement.

In direct conflict with the acknowledged existence of these valuable mining rights, the mine expropriation bill introduced in the Chilean Senate by President Allende provided specifically that there would be no right to any indemnification for the mineral deposits being exploited or planned eventually to be exploited in the future. The Constitutional Amendment provides that "no right to compensation shall be allowed for rights to mineral deposits." The amendment and implementing decree provide that El Teniente's mineral rights pass immediately to the Chilean State without, in the words of the legislation, "further formality."

Finally, the Chilean expropriation legislation declares "null and void" the advisory and management contracts between the joint mining companies and foreign parties even though these agreements may have substantial value to the companies. Again, there is no provision to compensate for the value of any interest lost by virtue of canceling these contracts.

2. Limitation to Book Value of Compensation in Respect of Other Assets

Under the Constitutional amendment, non-excluded assets are to be compensated for on the basis of their depreciated cost "book values" at December 31, 1970. No recognition is given to the fact that these assets have substantial additional value as part of a going concern. Thus, nothing in the legislation recognizes the past, current and future income potential of the mining companies, including El Teniente, the accepted standards of valuing mining properties.

Original cost figures, of course, do not approach going concern value. This is not surprising. The costs of assets acquired in past years will not reflect replacement costs, appreciation by reason of inflation, scarcity and other factors. Balance sheets do not reflect ore reserves or the intangible value of marketing practices, contracts, technical expertise, experience and the like. No express provision is made in the Chilean legislation to reflect any of these components of going concern value. This is the most fundamental defect in the Chilean legislation in terms of the compensation payable for expropriation under generally accepted principles of international law.

The departure between original cost less depreciation allowed for tax purposes and real or going concern value, is, of course, far greater in the case of a mining property which has been in operation for an extended period of time than in the case of a mining property which is relatively new or in the case of other businesses which have relatively short-lived assets or assets whose depreciated costs approach current values. Thus, in the case of some businesses, application of provisions in the expropriation legislation might not produce a result which would be a major departure from accepted international compensation standards.

Somewhat the same result *may* be achieved in El Teniente's case *if* the values which are shown on El Teniente's book are recognized and accepted as they have been consistently by the Chilean authorities over the years. Those values bear some relationship to the real values of the assets today because they incorporate the results of the 1965 appraisal of American Appraisal Company which brought asset values up to date as of that time. Assets acquired since that appraisal are no doubt undervalued because the effects of inflation are not reflected on El Teniente's books. However, the acceptance of book figures at December 31, 1970, would approach the true value of El Teniente as a going concern.

One provision in the expropriation legislation could be interpeted and applied to prevent this result. This provision requires that revaluations made by the joint companies or their predecessors since 1964 be disregarded. If this provision is interpreted to apply to arbitrary revaluations by personnel of these companies or revaluations to reflect changes in currency exchange rates as distinct from independent, authoritative, accepted valuations to bring book figures into line with actual values, the provision would not require adjustment of the book figures of El Teniente and so would not stand in the way of an appropriate compensation award. But if the provision is interpreted and applied to negate the effects of the 1965 El Teniente appraisal it would require reversion to wholly outdated original cost figures bearing no relationship to going concern or real asset values as required by accepted international law principles.

In his testimony before the Senate Commission, Chilean Professor Jorge Ovalle Quiroz concluded that paying for expropriated properties by using book values, deducting amortization made for tax purposes and excluding revaluation would result in "expropriation without compensation." Professor Ovalle, responding to certain international law decisions cited to support the pending legislation during the Senate Commission's debate, stated that the "only nationalizations without compensation" which he "knew" were "those which implied a seizure as a war penalty." The Chilean State's expropriation of the Gran Mineria would clearly not fall within this limited exception and would, therefore, be valid under international law only if prompt, adequate and effective compensation is paid for the expropriated enterprises.

3. Reduction of Compensation by Amount of "Excess Profits" Since 1955

Under the Constitutional amendment, the Chilean President is empowered to order the Comptroller General to reduce the total compensation due for the expropriated property of the joint mining companies by "all or part of the excess profits earned annually by the nationalized companies and their predecessors . . . [since 1955] giving special consideration to the normal profitability they have obtained in their international operations as a whole, or to agreements which the Chilean State may have concluded on the matter of maximum profitability of foreign companies established in the country." In explaining this provision to the Senate Commission, Mr. Novoa, the Chilean President's Legal Adviser, stated that the reasons for the "ceiling on compensation" created by the "excess profits" provision were "political matters." He failed to provide any basis in law for the provision other than a bare assertion that companies which "obtained profits above normal" should have the amount of such profits deducted from their compensation for expropriated properties.

The precise basis for calculating such reductions remains unclear. In his message accompanying the legislation as proposed, President Allende spoke of "excess profits" since 1955 "over and above the normal rate of profit . . . earned in . . . overall international operations." In a newspaper advertisement which appeared in the January 25, 1971, issue of *The New York Times* signed by the Corporacion del Cobre, it was explained that the deduction would correspond "to a compensation, though only in part, for the excessive returns which these [foreign] companies enjoyed by comparison with the works they maintained in other countries . . . ."[74]

The advertisement presented charts with figures which purported to compare the percentage of investment in Chile by two major mining companies with their worldwide investments and the per-

---

[74] N.Y. Times, Jan. 25, 1971, at 72–73, cols. 1–8.

centage of their profits realized in Chile with their worldwide profits. The advertisement did not explain how these figures were determined, nor did it indicate on what basis these figures would be used in determining the alleged "excess profits."

Under the expropriation legislation, the Chilean President is empowered to order the Comptroller General to consider in reducing the compensation by such "excess profits" the "standards agreed on between the State and the nationalized companies with respect to preferential dividends for . . . [Codelco] when the price for . . . [copper] has risen above the levels established by these same standards . . . ."[75] Again, there is no specification of how these standards would be used in making this reduction.

In the case of Braden's profits from the El Teniente mine from 1955 to the formation of the joint mining company and from the joint company, it is possible to make only a rough calculation of the effect of the "excess profits" provision on the compensation to which Braden would be entitled. There would be no "excess profits" realized by Braden if the calculation under the legislation were by comparing Braden's after-tax profit per pound of copper produced by El Teniente since 1955 with that of copper produced by Kennecott outside Chile.

The provision on "excess profits" has no foundation in generally accepted principles of international law as recognized by the United States. There was no "excess profits" under the laws of Chile in effect at the time profits were earned and dividends paid. The insertion of an excess profits recapture provision in the expropriation legislation is tantamount to confiscation unless that provision is found to be inapplicable under the circumstances.

4. Reduction of Compensation by Amount of Third Party Debt Proceeds Deemed Not "Usefully Invested"

Under the expropriation legislation it appears that creditors of the jointly owned mining companies would obtain the monies owing them from the compensation that the companies in question are to receive, unless Chile assumes these debts itself and, presumably, reduces the compensation award by the amount so assumed. The legislation provides that the State may choose not to assume debts whose proceeds are determined by the state not to have been "usefully invested."

[75] *Id.*

Not being competent to pass upon Chilean law, we do not presume to express an opinion as to the meaning or effect of this provision. If the meaning is that the Chilean government may not only decline to assume the obligations of the nationalized companies but is authorized to reduce the compensation payable for the taking, out of which the creditors are to be paid, any action taking advantage of this authorization would constitute an indirect abrogation of contract. If the meaning and effect go further and undertake to excuse the government on its obligations on the guarantees of payment of loans contracted by the nationalized companies, any action taking advantage of this would constitute a direct breach of contract which would constitute a violation of international law so serious as to undermine Chile's credit standing.

Neither the Chilean legislation nor its history contains any standards as to what constitutes a "usefully employed" debt incurred by a joint mining company. In the Senate Commission debate on the Chilean legislation the government representative, Mr. Max Nolff, Vice President of Codelco, refused to indicate which obligations Chile would not assume. If the "usefully employed" test is applied to reduce the expropriation award to less than the full, going concern value of El Teniente, the result will not be in accordance with generally accepted principles of international law.

5. Reduction of Compensation by Amount of Payments Under Repudiated Pre-Allende Equity-Purchase Agreements

Compensation provided for under the Chilean legislation will be reduced by an amount equal to "payments which the Corporacion del Cobre, Corporacion de Fomento de la Produccion, or the State of Chile have made or hereafter make, as the price for shares of stock bought by Chilean agencies or by virtue of the guaranties stipulated for the said price payment obligation . . . ." In addition "[a]ny stipulations regarding prices in commitments to buy shares agreed on with members of the mixed corporations, their form and terms of payment, and the principal and subsidiary obligations originating in those commitments to buy shares, and the promissory notes issued in connection therewith, insofar as they accord to the members or shareholders of the nationalized companies more rights than . . . [the right to receive a proportional share of compensation to the expropriated companies], shall be null and void."

According to President Allende's message accompanying the bill, these provisions are "obviously and generally speaking, an application of the permanent reform concerning the contract-laws." If they are applied to the 1967 agreement whereunder Braden sold its 51 per cent interest in El Teniente to Codelco, the effect would be to disregard the existence of El Teniente as a jointly owned company for purposes of computing the amounts of compensation due, to treat Braden as retaining its full ownership of El Teniente and to regard payments made for the sale of its 51 per cent interest to Codelco as, in effect, advance payments of compensation for expropriation. By this means Chile would nullify the pre-Allende sale agreement even though the contract-laws conferring authority to enter into such agreements were enacted pursuant to well-established Chilean practice and authority. Chilean Professor Ovalle, speaking during the Senate Committee's proceedings, characterized the failure to honor these agreements which were approved in valid Chilean contract laws as "a most reprehensible abuse." The professor pointed out that it was "not understandable" how the parties having rights under these contract-laws could be told by the Chilean State "that the law gave them this right, that they acquired it pursuant to the law and nevertheless it is illegal . . . ."

The effect of the repudiation of prior agreements, if interpreted in the manner described above and applied to the taking of Braden's interest in El Teniente, would be to reduce the compensation award payable to Braden in respect of its 49 per cent equity interest if the 1970 year-end book value of the eligible net assets of El Teniente determined under the legislative provision, less any excess profits, is less than $159 million. For example, if the net assets less excess profits were $130 million, the retroactive repudiation would reduce the award from $64 million (49 per cent of $130 million) to $50 million ($130 million less $80 million). On the other hand, the award would be increased under this analysis, if the adjusted book value of El Teniente's assets, but for the repudiation of prior agreements, would be more than $159 million, as would certainly be the case if actual and realistic asset values are to be applied. In these circumstances, repudiation of prior agreements could increase the expropriation award. For example, the net book value of assets at December 31, 1970, adding back dividends declared but not paid, was $362,400,000. This figure less $80 million would result in a compensation award of $282,400,000 which is substantially in excess of 49 per cent of $362,400,000.

Like the retroactive determination of "excess profits," the repudiation of prior sale agreements, made in accordance with laws valid at the time and *fully performed by both parties,* would be a clear departure from the accepted principle of awarding just compensation for expropriated properties. There is no precedent in international law for computing compensation for expropriated properties in this fashion.

If, on the other hand, the legislation is interpreted so as to apply the repudiation provision only to *prospective* payments to be made under prior agreements, this result may be avoided in the case of El Teniente. This is because the El Teniente purchase agreement now has been fully performed.

6. Possible Reduction of Real Value of Compensation Award by Deferral of Payment

The Chilean expropriation legislation requires payment "in legal tender unless the nationalized companies agree to another form of payment." These payments would be made over a term of "not . . . more than 30 years" and with interest of "not . . . less than 3 per cent."

These provisions for payment would permit the receipt of compensation for expropriated property to be deferred over a long period of time and would permit an interest rate which would not be realistic in determining the present value of any compensation award. It is inconceivable that an obligation bearing a rate of interest of as low as 3 per cent could be sold at anything approaching its face value.

President Allende's message to the Senate accompanying his bill stated that payment "may have to be made in hard currency or in national currency at the prevailing rate of exchange." The legislation as approved requires only that the payment be made in "legal tender." On March 14, 1971, Chilean Ambassador to the United States Orlando Letelier stated that compensation would be paid in hard currency if the initial investment in the expropriated enterprise was in hard currency.[76] In an interview published in *The Washington Evening Star* on May 20, 1971, Chilean President Allende is quoted as giving the following response to a question concerning how the United States copper companies would be compensated for their expropriated properties: "We have said they will be compensated and this can be in copper, which is the same as money, or in dollar bonds. The details are still being worked out."[77]

[76] Washington Evening Star, March 15, 1971, § A, at 3, cols. 4–5.
[77] Washington Evening Star, May 20, 1971, § A, at 2, cols. 1–4.

IV. CONCLUSION

The foregoing discussion demonstrates that the expropriation of Braden's interest in El Teniente pursuant to provisions of the Chilean Constitutional amendment could have the effect of denying to Braden the prompt, adequate and effective compensation for its interest in El Teniente to which Braden is entitled under generally accepted principles of international law as recognized by the United States and other nations. Those principles require that Braden be compensated for its interest in El Teniente in an amount which is not less than the value of that interest as part of a going concern. Any award by Chile for Braden's equity interest in El Teniente of less than $176 million would, we submit, fall below the generally accepted international legal standard of compensation for expropriation.

CHAPTER VI

International Law and the Chilean Nationalizations: The Valuation of the Copper Companies

Richard B. Lillich

T HE legal standards established by Chile to govern its nationalization of United States copper companies, discussed in the preceding chapter, came as something of a surprise, jurisprudentially at least. Unlike several other countries, whose recent nationalizations seriously challenge the international law principle of compensation,[1] Chile "made every effort to disarm its critics by recognizing the right in principle of the foreign investor to recover the value of his nationalized property, but reserving for scrupulous later analysis the question of amount. . . ."[2] Indeed, even a cursory examination of the Constitutional Amendment Concerning Natural Resources and Their Nationalization of July 15, 1971,[3] reveals the accuracy of the *New York Times'* characterization of President Allende as "a radical with a flair for legal niceties. . . ."[4] Although subsequent rhetoric, most notably portions of the President's Decree Concerning Excess Profits of Copper Companies of September 28, 1971,[5] somewhat beclouds the issues, the legal standards governing

---

[1] Leigh, *Book Review*, 40 GEO. WASH. L. REV. 582, 587 (1972). Even Friedmann, certainly no apologist for Western economic interests, acknowledged that some recent nationalization measures amount to "open or disguised confiscation. The clearest case of confiscation . . . was the nationalisation of American-owned sugar refineries by Cuba in 1960." Friedmann, *General Course in Public International Law* (Hague Academy of International Law), 127 RECUEIL DES COURS 39, 178 (1969–II).

[2] Rogers, *Foreword* to THE VALUATION OF NATIONALIZED PROPERTY IN INTERNATIONAL LAW at viii (R. Lillich ed. & contrib. 1972).

[3] The Constitutional Amendment is reprinted in 10 INT'L LEGAL MATERIALS 1067 (1971).

[4] N.Y. Times, Oct 3, 1971, § E., at 3, col. 6.

[5] The Decree is reprinted in 10 INT'L LEGAL MATERIALS 1235 (1971). Its flavor is reflected in the following paragraph: "On this occasion of determining the amount of compensation to correspond to the nationalization, after decades of exploitation the people of Chile now assert their right to have the principles of equity applied in favor of the national community. In the preservation of their patrimony, in the defense of their inherent right of economic sovereignty— historically violated by the copper enterprises—the people of Chile have earned their rights against these companies, which today they legally and logically exercise by deducting the excessive profits obtained by the nationalized enterprises." *Id.* at 1237.

the recent nationalizations and the methods of valuing the assets of the companies taken thereunder are susceptible of legal analysis and serious critique to an extent that the Cuban nationalizations, for instance, were not.[6]

These legal standards, it is fair to say, introduce "a variety of new legal concepts that reduce the potential valuation of the properties."[7] In the first place, the Comptroller General of Chile, who is made responsible for determining the amount of compensation that should be paid, is required to base his valuation solely upon "the book value as of December 31, 1970,"[8] less certain deductions to be mentioned briefly below.[9] Exclusive reliance upon book value, of course, occasionally may permit a just result in a given nationalization.[10] Generally, as a speaker at the Annual Meeting of the American Society of International Law in 1968 graphically demonstrated, such is not the case.[11] In the case of the copper companies, the constitutionally mandated use of the book value test, to the exclusion of other more reliable methods of valuation, has produced a compensation figure arguably below the amount required by international law.

---

[6] The Cuban nationalizations, "based upon a totally illusory funding system and payable in bonds that were never printed," so patently violated international law that serious analysis was unnecessary. *See* Dawson, *Current Decisions,* 8 A.B.A. Int'l & Comp. L. Bull. No. 2, at 28, 33 (1964). *Accord,* Friedmann, note 1 *supra.*

[7] N.Y. Times, Feb. 3, 1971, at 2, col. 5.

[8] The Constitutional Amendment, *supra* note 3, at 1068. Additionally, "[t]he amount of the compensation . . . shall be determined on the basis of the original cost of such assets, less amortization, depreciation, write-offs (castigos), and devaluation through obsolescence." *Id.* at 1067.

[9] *See* text at notes 27–39 *infra.*

[10] The difference between book value and "real or going concern value is, of course, far greater in the case of a mining property which has been in operation for an extended period of time than in the case of a mining property which is relatively new or in the case of other businesses which have relatively short-lived assets or assets whose depreciated costs approach current values. Thus, in the case of some businesses, application of provisions in the expropriation legislation might not produce a result which would be a major departure from accepted international compensation standards." *An Analysis of the Expropriation of the Properties of Sociedad Minera El Teniente by Chile in the Light of International Law Principles, supra* Chapter V, at 113 [hereinafter cited as Analysis].

[11] While the book value of General Motors Corporation at the end of 1962 was $6,367,407,221, the market value of its shares was over $17 billion. Panel Discussion, *The Taking of Property: Evaluation of Damages,* 62 Am. Soc'y Int'l L. Proceedings 35, 38 (1968) (Reeves). On the general inadequacy of book value as a measure of compensation, see McCosker, *Book Values in Nationalization Settlements,* Chapter III *supra.*

The long-standing position of the United States, reiterated recently by Whiteman, is that "[i]n the case of an operating enterprise, adequate compensation is usually considered to be an amount representing the market value or 'going concern' value of the enterprise, calculated as if the expropriation or other governmental act decreasing the value of the business had not occurred and was not threatened."[12] This position accords with such international precedents as the *Lena Goldfields* arbitration, where the value of a nationalized mining enterprise was based upon its "fair purchase price as a going concern."[13] The Foreign Claims Settlement Commission of the United States, with probably more experience valuating nationalized companies than any other tribunal, has rejected arguments that it rigidly apply the book value test.[14] In *Claim of the First National Bank of Boston*,[15] for instance, it ignored its previous presumption in favor of book value and rendered its decision on a going concern basis. The Commission held that

the nature of the business conducted is such that earnings potential reflected in the market price of the stock is of greater significance than asset value in the determination of true value of the enterprise at any given time. The Commission is persuaded that at the time of loss the claimant's six Cuban branches had a value exceeding their book value. . . .[16]

Subsequent decisions of the Commission frequently use the capitalization of earnings method of determining going concern value, applying a multiple of from 10^{17} to 15^{18} to the annual net earnings after taxes. In *Claim of Sun Oil Co.*,[19] a special mining concession case, it even adopted a multiple of $16\frac{2}{3}$.

The fact that the book value approach generally produces figures lower than the above methods of valuation lends credence to the statement by Charles A. Meyer, Assistant Secretary of State for Inter-American Affairs, that for a going concern the book value

[12] 8 M. WHITEMAN, DIGEST OF INTERNATIONAL LAW 1143 (1967).

[13] Quoted from Analysis at 99. *See generally* Nussbaum, *The Arbitration Between Lena Goldfields, Ltd., and the Soviet Government*, 36 CORNELL L.Q. 31 (1950).

[14] *See* Lillich, *The Valuation of Nationalized Property by the Foreign Claims Settlement Commission*, in THE VALUATION OF NATIONALIZED PROPERTY IN INTERNATIONAL LAW, *supra* note 2, at 95, 105–15.

[15] FCSC, ANN. REP. 33 (1969).   [16] *Id.* at 36.

[17] Claim of General Dynamics Corp., Dec. No. CU–3787 (Aug. 27, 1969).

[18] Claim of Colgate-Palmolive Co., Dec. No. CU–4547 (Feb. 3, 1971). A summary of the decision appears in Evans (ed.), *Judicial Decisions Involving Questions of International Law*, 65 AM. J. INT'L L. 627 (1971).

[19] Dec. No. CU–4706 (April 8, 1970).

test may be "a dubious measure of true worth. . . ."[20] Since, as William Blake is purported to have warned, "to generalize is to be an idiot," prudence dictates that Meyer's statement be tested in the Chilean context. In contrast to most nationalizations, where firm data is hard to come by, here the Kennecott Copper Corporation, and to some extent, the Republic of Chile, have made ample information available from which at least tentative conclusions may be drawn.

According to the Comptroller General, as of December 31, 1970, the basic book value of the El Teniente Mining Company, a 49 percent owned subsidiary of Kennecott, was approximately $365 million,[21] a figure the company appears willing to accept.[22] Moreover, Kennecott has acknowledged that it is "approximately the same figure derived by applying the customary valuation tests for mineral properties as going concerns. . . ."[23] Although it has called this figure "conservative,"[24] pointing out that by applying "realistic capitalization multiples to the over $20 million dividends . . . the going concern value for El Teniente based on earnings would be something on the order of $1 billion,"[25] Kennecott has made no real attempt to substantiate the latter valuation, and the impression exists that it could live with book value compensation despite its general inadequacy under international law.[26]

The Comptroller General, however, reduced the book value figure to $319 million, deducting from the balance sheet items for payment of retirement indemnization to workers,[27] for contributions to

[20] N.Y. Times, Oct. 16, 1971, at 6, col. 6.

[21] Brief for Kennecott Copper Corporation, Special Copper Tribunal (Dec. 2, 1971), *reprinted in* KENNECOTT COPPER CORPORATION, CONFISCATION OF EL TENIENTE 9, 52 (Supp. No. 2 1972) [hereinafter cited as Brief].

[22] KENNECOTT COPPER CORPORATION, CONFISCATION OF EL TENIENTE 9 (Supp. 1971). The company earlier had claimed a book value of $362.4 million. Analysis at 109.

[23] *Id.* "Using the internationally-recognized standards for valuing mining property which were followed by the *Lena Goldfields* tribunal, the present value of Braden's 49 percent equity investment in El Teniente, reduced by the 30 per cent Chilean dividend tax, is estimated at $175,884,000, assuming a 15 per cent risk rate, a 4 per cent safe or redemption rate, and a $.24 cost / price spread for copper." *Id. See* text at note 13 *supra.*

[24] *Id. Compare* text accompanying note 26 *infra.*

[25] *Id.* "Even this figure does not take into account the increased profitability of El Teniente based upon the 1967–1972 expansion program which, although substantially accomplished by early 1971, had not been reflected in actual production increases through 1970." *Id.*

[26] Indeed, it has stated that "the acceptance of book figures at December 31, 1970, would approach the true value of El Teniente as a going concern." *Id.* at 113. *Compare* text at note 24 *supra.*

[27] *See* Brief 10–12.

the cost of constructing houses for company personnel,[28] and for the difference in value of mining deposits.[29] These deductions, which were appealed unsuccessfully to a Special Copper Tribunal, may or may not be permissible modifications under good accountancy principles, but surely if such deductions are allowed from book value then additions, say for appreciation by reason of inflation, should be permitted too. The one-sidedness of Chile's invocation of the book value approach, even more than its general inadequacy, brings the Comptroller General's $319 million valuation perilously close to minimal compensation.

The provisions in the Constitutional Amendment authorizing the Comptroller General to subtract from this reduced book value compensation "any revaluations made by . . . [the] companies or their predecessors after December 31, 1964,"[30] plus "those amounts representing assets that the State fails to receive in good operating condition,"[31] have been utilized to deduct $198 million for revaluations and $21 million for deficient installations,[32] reducing the balance of compensation due Kennecott to $100 million. Both these deductions, also appealed unsuccessfully to the Special Copper Tribunal,[33] conceivably could be justified as relevant to the determination of adequate compensation, but they are subject to the same general criticism leveled at the first three deductions.

Finally, and this provision may be regarded as the proverbial straw that broke the camel's back, the Constitutional Amendment specifically empowered the President of Chile to order the Comptroller General, in computing the compensation, to deduct alleged "excess profits" retroactive to 1955.[34] According to Kennecott, "[t]he provision on 'excess profits' has no foundation in generally accepted principles of international law as recognized by the United States. There were no 'excess profits' under the laws of Chile in effect at the time profits were earned and dividends paid. The insertion of an excess profits recapture provision in the expropriation legislation is tantamount to confiscation unless that provision is found to be inapplicable under the circumstances."[35] Unfortunately for the company, President Allende found it applicable and ordered the Comp-

---

[28] *See* Brief 13–15.   [29] *See* Brief 14–15.

[30] The Constitutional Amendment, *supra* note 3, at 1069.   [31] *Id.*

[32] The Comptroller General's Resolution on Compensation of October 11, 1971, is reprinted in 10 INT'L LEGAL MATERIALS 1240 (1971). *See id.* at 1252 for the deductions given in the text.

[33] *See* Brief 16–41.

[34] The Constitutional Amendment, *supra* note 3, at 1069.

[35] Analysis at 115.

troller General to deduct $410 million from Kennecott's compensation balance of $100 million,[36] leaving the company with no prospects of any compensation whatsoever.[37] Since the alleged "excess profits" exceeded Kennecott's earnings from Chile during the fifteen-year period,[38] it is hard to construe the provision and the President's action under it as anything but nationally authorized international confiscation. This characterization, uncharitable as it may sound, finds support in the fact that there was no appeal from the President's order to the Special Copper Tribunal, much less to the regular courts of law.[39]

In sum, Chile, by recognizing its obligation to pay adequate compensation to foreigners for their nationalized property, initially inspired the hope that a Marxist regime in a country with a strong legal tradition could reorder its economy without provoking an international uproar that would redound to its own economic and political detriment. Although some of the provisions in the Constitutional Amendment governing the nationalization of the copper companies considerably dimmed this hope, it has been extinguished, in the eyes of many observers, by what the *New York Times* rightly called President Allende's "bizarre bookkeeping maneuver" over "excess profits."[40] Unhappily, his action in this regard created a political storm which obscures the important issues concerning the valuation of nationalized property raised, if not yet answered, by the Chilean nationalizations.

[36] President's Decree, *supra* note 5, at 1240.

[37] Comptroller General's Resolution, *supra* note 32, at 1253. Since no compensation is likely to be paid in the event, it is unnecessary to consider whether the form of payment contemplated, "the term not to exceed 30 years, and the interest not to be less than 3 percent per annum," complies with international law. The Constitutional Amendment, *supra* note 3, at 1069.

[38] KENNECOTT COPPER CORPORATION, CONFISCATION OF EL TENIENTE 4 (Supp. 1971).

[39] The Constitutional Amendment, *supra* note 9, at 1069. The companies tried to raise the excess profits question before the Special Copper Tribunal but met with no success. N.Y. Times, Sept. 8, 1972, at 45, col. 6; N.Y. Times, Sept. 9, 1972, at 29, col. 3. Its decision is reprinted in 11 INT'L LEGAL MATERIALS 1013 (1972).

[40] N.Y. Times, Oct. 2, 1971, at 28, col. 2.

Transmutation of Municipal Law Standards

CHAPTER VII

Real Property Valuations in Argentina, Chile, and Mexico

Robert K. Goldman and John M. Paxman

IN THE last decade, Latin America[1] has experienced constant political upheaval, frustration over the lack of dynamism in the region's economic development, initiation of vast programs to achieve greater social and distributive justice, and an acute population explosion which threatens to wipe out the social and economic progress achieved to date. This overall situation has contributed to a resurgence of economic nationalism throughout the hemisphere. The principal target of this nationalistic sentiment has been the foreign investor, who is popularly regarded as the cause of all the region's ills and the manipulator of its political and economic destiny. It is not surprising, therefore, that this sentiment had fostered a general pattern of property seizures[2] beginning in the 1960's. Contrary to popular belief, not all of these expropriations have affected foreign interests.[3] The domestic reforms of the past

---

[1] In using the term *Latin America* the following should be kept in mind. Latin America does not exist as an entity. Despite certain similarities between the twenty countries, they differ greatly due to geographical, cultural, racial, and political factors. Because of colonial experiences there is a general distrust of centralized government and institutionalized legal systems. Yet, oddly, there is a tendency to relegate the task of ordering society to the government. In this regard, see Dawson, *International Law, National Tribunals and the Rights of Aliens: The Latin American Experience*, 21 VAND. L. REV. 712 (1968). Similar sentiments are echoed by Manuel Angulo in his remarks in FOREIGN INVESTMENT IN LATIN AMERICA: PAST POLICIES AND FUTURE TRENDS 23–24 (Proceedings of Regional Meeting of American Society of International Law, Mar. 13, 14, 1970, publ. by VA. J. INT'L L. 1970). *See also* Bomchil, *Foreign Investment in Argentina*, in PRIVATE INVESTORS ABROAD: PROBLEMS AND SOLUTIONS IN INTERNATIONAL BUSINESS IN 1969, at 331 (1969).

[2] This term is used frequently in literature concerning expropriation. *See, e.g.,* E. MOONEY, FOREIGN SEIZURES: SABBATINO AND THE ACT OF STATE DOCTRINE (1967). The recent illegal takeovers of farms by tenant farmers in Chile most closely resemble property seizures.

[3] Major instances of expropriation of land and industrial facilities have occurred as follows: Argentina: oil concessions (1963); Bolivia: oil (1970); Brazil: oil refineries, land, and public utilities (1959–60); Chile: copper mines and land (1964, 1969, 1971); Colombia: land (1962); Cuba: total expropriation (1959–61); Mexico: land and public utilities (1960); Peru: land, oil, and public utilities (1968–70). For an expanded look at the circumstances surrounding

decade also have brought about a marked change in the distribution
and control of real property held by nationals.[4]

I. INTRODUCTION

It is, of course, apparent that any attempt to implement comprehensive social, political, and economic reforms depends upon the
availability of standardized legal powers. Such powers by their very
nature may be exercised subject to the limits imposed by the domestic sovereign jurisdiction and the international legal order. The
power to expropriate is an example of the combined effect of these
restraining forces. In reforming land tenure patterns, many Latin
American nations have relied on their expropriatory authority in
taking real property. When foreign interests are affected, international law has placed certain limitations upon the exercise of
this authority. As a rule, the exercise of the expropriatory power is
entirely proper and acceptable according to customary international
law so long as certain minimal criteria are met.[5] Generally, the
expropriation must be nondiscriminatory,[6] consistent with the ap-

---

these expropriations, see Comment, *Argentina and the Hickenlooper Amendment,* 54 CALIF. L. REV. 2078 (1966); Note, *The Threat to U.S. Private Investment in Latin America,* 5 J. INT'L L. & ECONOMICS 221 (1971); Thome, *Expropriation in Chile Under the Frei Agrarian Reform,* 19 AM. J. COMP. L. 489
(1971); Jaramillo, *Expropriación Forzosa y la Ley de Reforma Agraria y Co-
lonización del Ecuador,* 12 REVISTA DE DERECHO ESPAÑOL Y AMERICANO 55
(1967); Lumpkin, *Gulf Oil's Experience in Bolivia,* 8 HOUSTON L. REV. 472
(1971); Palacios, *Doctrina: Brea y Parinas,* 27 REVISTA DE JURISPRUDENCIA PE-
RUANA 251 (1969). For a report of property takings in Latin America and for
an account of which claims have been settled, see U.S. Department of State
Report on Nationalization, Expropriation, and Other Takings of U.S. and
Certain Foreign Property Since 1960 reprinted in 11 INT'L LEGAL MATERIALS 84–
119 (1972). *See also* K. KATZAROV, THE THEORY OF NATIONALIZATION 42–73
(1964) for a summary of property takings from the commencement of World
War II to 1963.

[4] The principal force in this regard has been the far-reaching agrarian reform
systems that have been instituted in many countries. *See* Thome, note 3 *supra.*

[5] Wortley, *Expropriation in International Law,* THE GROTIUS SOCIETY: TRANS-
ACTIONS FOR THE YEAR 1947, at 30 (1948). Wortley asserts that any state may
expropriate in accordance with its own system of law through the powers of
either its legislative, judicial, or executive branches of government.

[6] 2 D. O'CONNELL, INTERNATIONAL LAW 854, 855 (1965). In the lower court
decision in Banco Nacional de Cuba v. Sabbatino, 193 F. Supp. 375 (D.C.N.Y.
1961), *rev'd on other grounds,* 376 U.S. 398 (1964), it was observed that expropriation based solely upon the fact that the property was owned by aliens
is deemed to be a violation of this condition.

plicable domestic and international law,[7] and entail just compensation.[8] Nevertheless, recourse to the expropriatory power is an invitation for potential abuse. The critical question in expropriation situations is whether the legal remedies afforded to persons affected by the property takings are adequate both under domestic and international standards. Under the minimum standards, nations must provide a semblance of adequate judicial and administrative machinery for the settlement of disputes that may arise over valuation as a result of the authorized taking.[9] Moreover, the redress of grievances must be comparatively effective.[10] Compliance with this duty is a fundamental requirement of customary international law. If domestic procedural protections and guarantees fall short of the minimum standards, certain liabilities may attach, especially when foreigners are involved in the controversy. In short, the principal thrust of customary international practice has been to minimize abusive and arbitrary procedures in handling international claims.

The premise that a state should not be able to act in a discriminatory fashion cannot be seriously challenged. But, where property takings are concerned, there may be a tendency to disregard the requirements of justice and to deny even the most basic procedural safeguards. This is particularly true in light of the recognized supremacy of national interests over those of a purely individual nature.[11] Moreover, in the international legal order there is a

---

[7] This requirement is concerned with the basis for which the property is taken. To meet international as well as domestic standards, the expropriation must be based on public utility, security, or some other national interest. G.A. Res. 1803, 17 U.N. GAOR Supp. 17, at 15, U.N. Doc. A/5217 (1962).

[8] Article 4 of the U.N. Resolution on Permanent Sovereignty over Natural Resources states, in part, that in cases of expropriation "the owner shall be paid appropriate compensation. . . ." *Id.*

[9] G. SCHWARZENBERGER, A MANUAL OF INTERNATIONAL LAW 165 (4th ed. 1960).

[10] *Id.*

[11] Perhaps the most notable example of this awareness is the U.N. Resolution on Permanent Sovereignty over Natural Resources. Controversial Article 4 reads: "Nationalization, expropriation or requisitioning shall be based on ground or reasons of public utility, security or the national interest which are recognized as overriding purely individual or private interests, both domestic and foreign. In such cases the owner shall be paid appropriate compensation, in accordance with the rules in force in the State taking such measures in the exercise of its sovereignty and in accordance with international law. In any case where the question of compensation gives rise to a controversy, the national jurisdiction of the State, taking such measures shall be exhausted. However, upon agreement of sovereign States and other parties concerned, settlement of the dispute should be made through arbitration or international adjudication." *See* note 7 *supra.* For an inside view of events preceding the enactment of the resolution, *see*

notable friction between the acts of individual states and the requirements of the sometimes derisively termed "international standard."[12]

Aside from the question of the propriety of the expropriation,[13] which is not usually subject to challenge once a determination of public necessity has been made,[14] the most contentious issue traditionally has been that of compensation. The right to be compensated for the loss of property has been established as a basic principle of both municipal and international law[15] with the exception of the Communist-bloc countries.[16] However, a vigorous debate still centers on whether the compensation should be "full,"[17] "just,"[18] "ap-

Schwebel, *Story of the United Nations' Declaration on Permanent Sovereignty over Natural Resources*, 49 A.B.A.J. 463 (1963). *See also* Orrego, La Resolución 1803 de la Asamblea General de Las Naciones Unidas Sobre "Soberania Permanente Sobre los Recursos Naturales": Principios y Alcances de Derecho Internacional (Universidad de Chile, mimeo., 1971) for another view of that resolution's significance in the context of recent Chilean expropriation.

[12] The most notorious example of this friction is exemplified in Banco Nacional de Cuba v. Sabbatino, 376 U.S. 398 (1964), where the Supreme Court invoked the act of state doctrine and refused to review the expropriation acts of Cuba according to accepted international legal standards.

[13] Even though some authors argue that the word *expropriation* is necessarily ambiguous, the term will be employed throughout this article because it is the precise label given to state interference with private property rights in the Latin American systems analyzed herein. Dawson & Weston, *"Prompt, Adequate and Effective": A Universal Standard of Compensation?*, 30 Fordham L. Rev. 727 n.1 (1962).

[14] Once the decision has been made that state intervention for public benefit is necessary, there is no recourse against that determination; it is largely a political question. Lugui, *La Revisión de la Causa de Utilidad Pública en la Expropriación*, 128 La Ley, Revista Jurídica Argentina 1022, 1025 (1967) [hereinafter cited as La Ley].

[15] The Declaration on Permanent Sovereignty over National Resources, adopted in 1962, can be viewed as an attempt to codify this principle. "In such cases the owner shall be paid appropriate compensation, in accordance with the rules in force in the State taking such measures in the exercise of its sovereignty and in accordance with international law." *See* note 7 *supra*.

[16] There appears to be ample indication that their disavowal of a universal requirement of compensation is more theoretical than practical, for since World War II more than seventy-two agreements have been reached with Communist nations that apparently do not repudiate the principle of compensation. *See* Sweeney, *The Restatement of Foreign Relations Law of the United States and the Responsibility of States for Injury to Aliens*, 16 Syracuse L. Rev. 762, 768, 769 (1965); I. Foighel, Nationalization And Compensation 305 (1964); Seidl-Hohenveldern, *Communist Theories on Confiscation and Expropriation*, 7 Am. J. Comp. L. 541, 548 (1958).

[17] In negotiating lump sum settlements, the Department of State always seeks full compensation. 62 Am. Soc'y. Int'l L. Proceedings 42 (1968) [hereinafter

propriate,"[19] or "partial."[20] Unhappily, this adjectival debate has continued without consideration of the more technical methods employed to appraise the value of expropriated property and the standards governing evidence of value as accepted by domestic courts.[21] Even the most comprehensive studies have neglected to

---

cited as PROCEEDINGS]. Moreover, the RESTATEMENT (SECOND) OF FOREIGN RELATIONS LAW OF THE UNITED STATES § 188 (1) (d) (1965) takes the position that "full" compensation is the desirable standard. It is argued that the rule of subsection (1) (d) was enunciated by the Permanent Court of International Justice in the Case Concerning the Factory of Chorzow, [1927] P.C.I.J., ser. A, No. 17, at 47, where full value was equated with market value. Practical experience, however, belies the assertion that "full" compensation in the market value sense of the word is the international standard. A majority of the recoveries have been considerably less than the full amount demanded by the expropriated parties. For example, in the Mexican-American Agreement of 1941, which resolved all prior agrarian and other claims exclusive of the petroleum seizures, Mexico agreed to pay $40 million in installments, as against claims that totaled more than $350 million. *See* American-Mexican Claims Report, U.S. Dept. of State Pub. No. 2859, Arb. Ser. 9, at 4 (1948). With regard to the oil properties, the United States, acting on behalf of the oil companies who had estimated the value of their holdings at $260 million, settled for a sum of $24 million plus interest. For a précis of the final Mexican-American Agreement on oil expropriation, see 6 DEP'T STATE BULL. 351 (1942).

[18] A U.S.-Mexican agreement for compensation stated that the amount paid would reflect the "just value" of the expropriated property. *See* G. WHITE, NATIONALISATION OF FOREIGN PROPERTY 193 (1961). Also, the Draft Convention of the OECD on the Protection of Foreign Property employs the qualifier "just" to the concept of compensation. There just compensation is defined to "represent the genuine value of the property affected. . . ." 2 INT'L LEGAL MATERIALS 241, 248 (1963).

[19] *See* note 11 *supra*.

[20] One exponent of the international standard of justice suggests that the compensation rule be modified in certain instances: ". . . that a state is bound to respect the property of aliens . . . must be recognized in cases in which fundamental changes in the political and economic structures of the state or far-reaching social reforms entail interference, on a large scale, with private property. In such cases, neither the principle of absolute respect for alien property nor rigid equality with dispossessed nationals offer a satisfactory solution of the difficulty. *It is probable that, consistently with legal principle, such solution must be sought in granting partial compensation*" [emphasis added]. 1 OPPENHEIM, INTERNATIONAL LAW 352 (8th ed. Lauterpacht 1955).

[21] One noteworthy exception to the general situation concerning the question of international valuation procedures is the recent treatment given the subject in THE VALUATION OF NATIONALIZED PROPERTY IN INTERNATIONAL LAW (R. Lillich ed. & contrib. 1972). Moreover, Professor Lillich, in an earlier article, cites "the need to abjure sterile debates on the measure of compensation and begin attempts to formulate an international rule derived from the elements of damage allowed by municipal courts in condemnation proceedings." Lillich, *Toward the Formulation of an Acceptable Body of Law Concerning State Responsibility*,

analyze this facet of the expropriatory procedure. This neglect may stem from the complex multiplicity of factors that affect the valuation process; however, it detracts from the search to fashion an acceptable set of international rules.[22] Moreover, an explanation that valuation involves primarily nonlegal procedures is likewise unsatisfactory, for the ultimate task of the legal system, in instances of expropriation, is to give binding effect to the valuation, thereby creating a legal duty to compensate in the amount specified by valuation.[23] Even if the valuation is reached by mutual accord without recourse to the courts, the issue of valuation is a relevant subject of concern to international lawyers and scholars.

Although some rather important comparative studies have been made during the last decade,[24] the notable paucity of comment on the subject of real property valuation methods used in international practice has prompted the preparation of this chapter. The purpose of this essay is to review and analyze existing valuation practices and procedures in Mexico, Chile, and Argentina, and to determine whether these practices may serve as a basis for fashioning an acceptable international valuation standard.

---

16 SYRACUSE L. REV. 721 (1965). Lastly, see Freidberg, *A New Technique in the Adjudication of International Claims*, 10 VA. J. INT'L L. 282 (1970) for an enlightened view of what valuation criteria and procedures are acceptable to the Foreign Claims Settlement Commission of the United States. The four principal methods of valuation used by the FCSC are fair market value, book value, going concern value, and replacement cost.

[22] One also may accept the argument that such procedures are the province of the legal regimes of the individual sovereign nations, and as long as there is not a total denial of justice in such methods of disposition there is no reason for international concern. This point of view would be consistent with the language of the United Nations Declaration, *supra* note 7, which states that compensation shall be determined in "accordance with the rules in force in the State . . . and in accordance with international law." Since international valuation rules are vague, it may be assumed that the legal limits to acceptable valuation systems are to be governed principally by state practice.

[23] Alterini, *Indemnización Expropriatoria como obligación de Dar Sumas de Dinero*, 180 REVISTA JURÍDICA DE BUENOS AIRES 185 (1964).

[24] The Procedural Aspects of International Law Institute has been prominent in this field, having published the following series of books dealing with the subject matter at hand: R. LILLICH, INTERNATIONAL CLAIMS: THEIR ADJUDICATION BY NATIONAL COMMISSIONS (1962); R. LILLICH & G. CHRISTENSON, INTERNATIONAL CLAIMS: THEIR PREPARATION AND PRESENTATION (1962); R. FALK, THE ROLE OF DOMESTIC COURTS IN THE INTERNATIONAL LEGAL ORDER (1964); R. LILLICH, THE PROTECTION OF FOREIGN INVESTMENT: SIX PROCEDURAL STUDIES (1965); R. LILLICH, INTERNATIONAL CLAIMS: POSTWAR BRITISH PRACTICE (1967); B. WESTON, INTERNATIONAL CLAIMS: POSTWAR FRENCH PRACTICE (1971); F. DAWSON & I. HEAD, INTERNATIONAL LAW, NATIONAL TRIBUNALS AND THE RIGHTS OF ALIENS (1971).

II. THE SIGNIFICANCE OF VALUE

Since a determination of the monetary amount to be offered as compensation requires a unique judgment as to the worth of the taken property, some attempt should be made to define the nature of value and the process through which it is ascertained, *i.e.*, valuation. Value, in at least one instance, has been defined rather broadly in terms of the "criteria against which goals are chosen."[25] Although this definition is seemingly uneconomic in scope, it is still relevant to expropriated property valuation, especially when considered against the backdrop of the recent Chilean constitutional revision.[26] This definition implies that value is the result of competing priority judgments that may be measured from at least two basically antagonistic perspectives: that of the expropriator (governmental will) and that of the expropriated party (individual aspirations). It is not difficult to perceive the potential problems involved if a determination of value is made in favor of one party to the detriment of the other.[27] One readily could envision numerous instances where the exigencies of public utility and welfare could override the rights of individual citizens. On the other hand, the owner, if not legally restrained, may tend to inflate substantially claims relating to the property taken. In addition, there are always other relevant perspectives on questions of economic value. Therefore, under this approach, value ideally is determined by a combination of influencing factors, some advanced by the expropriator, some by the expropriated party, and some by less directly affected parties. But the rub arises from the purported balancing process, which is both difficult and delicate.[28]

[25] K. CARLSTON, LAW AND ORGANIZATION IN WORLD SOCIETY 43 (1962).

[26] *See infra* note 39, art. 10 (10) (4). The language of the Chilean Constitution now reads:

". . . the expropriated will always have the rights to be indemnified, the amount of which will be equitably determined by taking into consideration the interest of the community and those of the expropriated." *Id.*

[27] I. ORGEL, VALUATION UNDER THE LAW OF EMINENT DOMAIN §§ 12–14 (3d ed. 1953). Orgel suggests that neither the value to the taker nor the value to the owner suffices in expropriation proceedings. He therefore asserts that market value is the appropriate test for valuation purposes.

[28] The difficulty of making a property valuation is complicated when the act of expropriation affects property held by aliens, for in that instance interests that are international in scope also enter the process. The U.N. Resolution on Permanent Sovereignty over Natural Resources illustrates this by stating that the methods used to compute property value shall be made "in accordance with the rules in force in the State . . . and in accordance with international law." *Supra* note 7, art. 4.

Beyond the area of competing interests, any attempt to establish value is complicated by the fact that the value or worth of a given item may vary depending upon the purpose of valuation.[29] The most cursory analysis of pertinent material will reveal this to be true. Whether the valuation is for establishing the worth of a commercial inventory, providing insurance, determining loan security, indemnifying damages, affixing tax assessment, or assessing compensable claims, the value of the same property will vary accordingly.[30] Yet, in a purely theoretical sense, it has been argued that value should remain constant despite the purpose of the valuation:

The value of an immovable in a given moment is singular, whatever the purpose for which it is evaluated be. This value is ideal and the object of a valuation is to approximate, as near as is possible that ideal.[31]

The process of valuation also has been defined as the monetary estimation of the value of possessions,[32] as the art of establishing the just values of exchange of determined properties,[33] and as the estimation in monetary terms of the value of an indicated thing, always bearing in mind that the subject of the valuation can be assigned a value.[34] In other words, valuation involves translating the multifaceted worth of an item into numerical or monetary terms.

In expropriatory situations, the valuation process, in theory, should be based on an unencumbered mental operation whereby various persons—judges, appraisers, functionaries—utilize certain indexes, factors, and elements of judgment in order to estimate the value of the property in question. Obviously, this process gives to the persons who effectuate the valuation an ample degree of discretion.[35] Again, in the conceptual sense, the procedures of the *actual* valuation are, for the most part, very technical in nature and are not, therefore, subject to what may be called strict legal norms. Generally, the laws and codes of procedure that regulate the act of valuation itself do not attempt to establish specific technical guide-

[29] McMichael's Appraising Manual 6–7 (3d ed. 1945). The author lists nearly fifty varying types of property values that may be established depending on the purpose of valuation.

[30] E. Lapa, Estudio del Título de Propriedad / La Tasación de Inmuebles 132 (1968).

[31] This statement was prepared at the 1st Pan American Convention of Appraisers held in Lima, Peru, during 1949 and is cited by Lapa, *id.* at 132.

[32] L. Gronda, Curso de Economía Política y Sociales 24 (1946).

[33] *See* E. Lapa, *supra* note 30, at 129.   [34] Código Civil arts. 2311, 2312.

[35] *See* J. Oyhanarte, La Expropriación y los Servicios Púbjicos 78 (1957).

lines.[36] Rather, the development of such guidelines has been left to the customs of the assessors. In order to handle these technical procedures, specialized bodies, in many instances, have been formed.[37] The actual valuation, by necessity, must be made in the first instance by reference to rules of thumb that permit the comparison of the object to be appraised with others of a similar nature that have been valued through the use of similar techniques. However, factors that are not acceptable as evidence of value before the courts may not be included in the appraisal. Consequently, in the final analysis, the courts will determine whether the valuation conforms to established legal standards. They alone are empowered to settle conclusively disputes that arise from the valuation process.

III. ADMINISTRATIVE AND PROCEDURAL ASPECTS OF THE EXPROPRIATION PROCESS

A. CONSTITUTIONAL ASPECTS

In Argentina,[38] Chile,[39] and Mexico,[40] the power of the state to expropriate and the corollary right of affected parties to receive compensation in accordance with due procedures are constitutionally derived. Although relevant constitutional provisions by implication endow certain state agencies with expropriatory authority, they also guarantee the protection of the individual's property rights. Generally, the exercise of this expropriatory power depends on a finding by the proper administrative body that either public interest or necessity[41] requires the taking. The expropriated owner

[36] *See, e.g.,* the Argentine Code of Procedure, 100 LA LEY 557 (1962).

[37] *See* text at note 74 *infra.*

[38] CONSTITUTION OF ARGENTINA art. 17 (1853). The basis for the Argentine law of eminent domain is contained in this article of the Constitution, which states:

"Property is inviolable, and no inhabitant of the Nation can be deprived thereof except by virtue of judgment founded in law. Expropriation for public benefit must be authorized by law and previously compensated."

[39] CONSTITUTION OF CHILE art. 10(10) as amended by Law No. 16, 615 of January 18, 1967:

"No one may be deprived of his property except by virtue of a general or special law authorizing expropriation for reason of public utility or social interests."

[40] CONSTITUTION OF MEXICO art. 27 (1919):

"Expropriations can only be made by reason of public utility and by means of indemnity."

[41] It should be noted that the new Chilean provision permits taking for reasons based on "social interest." *See* note 26 *supra.*

is then entitled to indemnification for the monetary loss incurred as a result of the taking.[42] The scope of judicial review in most expropriation cases is severely limited by legislative acts. Courts normally lack jurisdiction to review the legality of the taking so long as the public interest motive is shown, on the ground that such a finding is a political act not cognizable by the judiciary.[43]

Since proceedings accompanying an expropriatory act are essentially administrative, recourse to the courts respecting methods of determining compensation can be avoided completely if the interested parties agree on the valuation of the property taken. However, if a dispute over the valuation exists, the courts may settle the

---

[42] It should also be noted that the constitutions of the countries in question vary on the question of whether compensation must precede the final act of taking. The Mexican Constitution of 1857 included guaranteed prior payment. However, the Constitution of 1919 eliminated that qualifying word in favor of the word *mediante,* which is more vague in nature. Some authorities argue that this was a conscious change to facilitate the widespread social reform of that era and that the constitutional requirement of prior payment is no longer the law. P. ROUAIX, GENESIS OF ARTICLES 27 AND 123 OF THE POLITICAL CONSTITUTION OF 1917, at 135–37 (1945) ; G. FRAGA, DERECHO ADMINISTRATIVO 414 (12th ed. 1968) . However, the general rule, absent a legislated policy to the contrary, appears to favor payment at the time the state takes possession of the property or as soon after as is practicable. Haas Hermanos y Cia, 56 SEMANARIO JUDICIAL DE LA FEDERACIÓN 1166 (1938) [hereinafter cited as S.J.F.]. Yet some Mexican Supreme Court decisions have tended to favor so-called deferred payment when there is both an urgent necessity for the expropriation and an inability of the government to pay immediately. Cia. Mexicana de Petroleo "El Aquila" S.A., 62 S.J.F. 3021 (1938) .

[43] G. FRAGA, DERECHO ADMINISTRATIVO 412 (12th ed. 1968) . Under Article 27 of the Mexican Constitution decisions to grant or restore communal lands within the Agrarian Reform scheme are specifically not subject to court review by use of the *amparo* suit, a suit to protect private persons from unconstitutional laws or illegal official acts. R. BAKER, JUDICIAL REVIEW IN MEXICO 132–38 (1971) . *See also* F. DAWSON & I. HEAD, INTERNATIONAL LAW, NATIONAL TRIBUNALS AND THE RIGHTS OF ALIENS 203–06 (1971) . A Chilean case, State (Fisco) v. Guzman Contreras, Supreme Court, May 24, 1960, 57 REVISTA DE DERECHO, JURISPRUDENCIA Y SCIENCIAS SOCIALES, Sec. I, at 83 (1960) [hereinafter cited as REV. SER. JURIS.], held that no court had the jurisdiction to review either whether the contemplated activity qualified as one being for the public benefit or whether the expropriated property was suitable for that purpose. And the Argentine courts have also abstained from examining the determination of public utility on the basis that the question was nonjusticiable in that such a finding is the result of a power vested exclusively in the legislature. Provincia de Jujuy v. Ledesma Sugar Estates & Refining Co., 209 FALLOS DE LA SUPREMA CORTE DE JUSTICIA DE LA NACIÓN 39 (1947 [hereinafter FALLOS]. *But see* Luigi, note 14 *supra. See also* Nación Argentina v. Jorge Ferrarion, 251 FALLOS 246 (1961) (automobile confiscation) , which held that the courts can review cases where the state takes property of a citizen and gives it to another for private use.

dispute by exercising their jurisdictional authority in accordance with applicable legislation. In Mexico and Chile for example, the courts' jurisdiction is limited usually to cases where there is no tax record of appraisal that can be used as evidence of value or where the value of taken property has appreciated or depreciated since the last tax valuation.[44] In all cases, the ultimate right to compensation, as well as procedures governing the calculation of value, is constitutionally guaranteed. These procedural protections are somewhat analogous to those afforded to claimants by the Fifth and Fourteenth Amendments in eminent domain actions in the United States.[45] It is interesting to note, however, that while valuation practices in the United States[46] were developed largely by the courts

[44] The Mexican Constitution states that the courts will intervene in the valuation process only in these instances or that this limited aspect of valuation will be the only area that "shall be subject to an expert judgment and a judicial resolution." Art. 27, para. 15. Under the Chilean Agrarian Reform Law, the Agrarian Tribunal operates under limits similar to those imposed in the Mexican scheme. Ley No. 16, 640, art. 42 (1967).

[45] The pertinent language of the Fifth Amendment is:

"No person shall . . . be deprived of life, liberty, or property, without due process of law; nor shall private property be taken for public use, without just compensation."

The requirement that the compensation be just is similar to those in some Latin American constitutions. CONSTITUTION OF BRAZIL art. 141, para. 16 (1946); art. 153, para. 22 (1967). The Argentine Constitution of 1819 provided that the owner of expropriated property "shall receive *just* compensation therefor." The Constitution of 1853 omitted the word *just*, but the omission is not thought to have diminished that standard due to the derivation of the Spanish word *indemnización* from the Latin *damnum* ("damage"). The idea is that the requirement that compensation be just is still implicitly present in the constitutional context. The object is to leave the expropriated party "without damage" through compensation. *See* Gordillo, *Argentina* in EXPROPRIATION IN THE AMERICAS 15, 19–20 (A. Lowenfeld ed. 1972) and Marienhoff, *"Justa" Indemnización: Concepto y Fundamento Positivo*, 4 REVISTA JURISPRUDENCIA ARGENTINA 255 (1959). Moreover, the Argentine Civil Code, which was adopted in 1869, still contains a provision which states:

"No one may be deprived of his property but for reason of public utility and by just compensation prior to transfer. In such case just compensation shall mean not only payment of the actual value of the property, but also direct damages resulting from the loss of the property." CÓDIGO CIVIL art. 2511.

Noteworthy is the use of the adjective "just," especially in view of the controversy that surrounds attempts to ascertain a more precise standard for compensation. *See* United States v. Lee, 106 U.S. 196 (1882).

[46] In the United States and other Anglo-American systems, these procedures have evolved over the years through judicial interpretation. Smith, *Real Property Valuation for Foreign-Wealth Deprivations*, in THE VALUATION OF NATIONALIZED PROPERTY IN INTERNATIONAL LAW 133, 144–67 (R. Lillich ed. & contrib. 1972).

on a case-by-case basis, they evolved in most Latin American nations by way of legislative enactments in the form of general or specific expropriation laws.[47] What follows is a general survey of valuation procedures and techniques in Mexico, Chile, and Argentina.

B. MEXICAN VALUATION PROCEDURES

The Mexican Law of Expropriation[48] sets forth a rather comprehensive scheme of valuation procedures. Except for extraordinary cases, the expropriating administrative authority determines the amount of compensation based on its valuation techniques.[49] Initially, the courts do not participate in the process, on the theory that the process of valuation is not a jurisdictional act[50] and, therefore, not within the powers of the judiciary. Since the basis for property valuation is rather rigidly fixed by law,[51] the courts do not play an important role in the preliminary stages of valuation. If the party seeking compensation agrees to the valuation of the expropriating agency, the courts are not required to intervene at all, as no justiciable issue is raised.[52]

Yet the judicial branch does have constitutionally derived authority to intervene when there is a controversy regarding the

[47] The promulgation of such laws is a means of asserting two principles of sovereignty: 1) control over foreign interests during periods of revolutionary internal reform, and 2) control over domestic national resources and economic systems. *See generally* A. GAITHER, EXPROPRIATION IN MEXICO (1940) ; A. CUELLAR, EXPROPRIACIÓN Y CRISIS EN MEXICO (1940) ; Pinto, *Political Aspects of Economic Development in Latin America*, in OBSTACLES TO CHANGE IN LATIN AMERICA 9 (C. Valiz ed. 1965) ; Frei & Trivelli, *Mensaje del Ejecutivo al Congreso Proponiendo la Aprobación del Projecto de la Ley de Reforma Agraria*, in VODANOVIC, LEY DE REFORMA AGRARIA 9 (1967) .

[48] Ley de Expropriación de 23 Noviembre de 1936 arts. 10–17 [hereinafter cited as Mexican Expropriation Law], Diario Oficial Nov. 25, 1936. The law had as its objectives the potential expropriation of movable and immovable goods or property, mercantile businesses, and industrial enterprises and the limitation of rights to property. A. ROJAS, DERECHO ADMINISTRATIVO 903 (2d ed. 1961) .

[49] Rojas, *La expropriación en el Derecho Mexicano*, 23 LA JUSTICIA, Dec. 1963, No. 404, at 51.

[50] G. FRAGA, DERECHO ADMINISTRATIVO 415 (12th ed. 1968) ; Mexican Expropriation Law art. 10.

[51] Mexican Expropriation Law art. 10. The Mexican Constitution fixes the value of the property as it appears in the tax records as the principal base for valuation of properties expropriated for public utility. Art. 27, para. 15.

[52] Where there is no controversy as to the amount of compensation there need be no judicial intervention. Case of Noriega Esperanza g. y Felix, Josefa y Amparo, 63 S.J.F. 4089 (1939) .

asserted valuation. The courts may intervene only in cases of appreciation or depreciation in value after the last fiscal valuation or in a case where the value of the expropriated property has not been noted on the registers of the tax office.[53] It also should be noted that either party may have recourse to the courts if that party has valid cause to do so.[54] The administrative body may desire to apply for expert appraisal and judicial determination when it considers that the value of the expropriated property as registered does not correspond to the present value; the owner may desire to seek the help of the courts when there have been improvements made to the property that create a basis for an appreciation in value of the property that has not been taken into account on the tax records.

In short, when a controversy concerning the amount of compensation arises, specifically if it is demonstrated that the amount does not conform to the limits set, the cause may be assigned for judicial resolution.[55] If the parties turn to the courts, each has the right to appoint an expert appraiser to represent him in the proceedings.[56] Failure to appoint a representative will result in the appointment of one by the judge. The appraisers then are given a period of sixty days in which to submit their opinions as to value. If the two appraisals are dissimilar and there is no agreement, the judge will order, according to law, that a third be made. The latter is generally viewed by the judge as being dispositive of the issue of value.[57] Lastly, there is no appeal from this judicial resolution of the valuation issue; *i.e.*, it is final and binding.[58] Nonappealability is imposed because all parties have been offered adequate opportunity

---

[53] *See* note 51 *supra*.

[54] E. Velasco, Análisis de la Ley de Expropriación Vigente: Derecho Comparado 22 (1956).

[55] Mexican Expropriation Law arts. 1–8; *See also* Código Federal de Procedimiento Civil arts. 521 *et seq.*

[56] *See supra* note 51, art. 11.

[57] *Id.* art. 16.

[58] *Id.* art. 17. A somewhat parallel practice is followed in the United States with regard to claims adjudicated by the Foreign Claims Settlement Commission: "The action of the Commission in allowing or denying any claim under this title shall be final and conclusive on all questions of law and fact and not subject to review by the Secretary of State or any other official, department, agency, or establishment of the United States or by any court by mandamus or otherwise." International Claims Settlement Act of 1949, as amended, 22 U.S.C. § 1623 (h) (1970). *See* Lillich, *Judicial Review and the FCSC*, 15 Admin. L. Rev. 72 (1963); Re, *The Foreign Claims Settlement Commission: Its Functions and Jurisdiction*, 60 Mich. L. Rev. 1079 (1962). For a case interpreting this section of the Act, see Tillman v. United States, 320 F.2d 396 (Ct. Cl. 1963).

and means to ascertain the value to their own satisfaction, especially with regard to appointment of experts.

C. CHILEAN VALUATION PROCEDURES

The Chilean constitutional revision of 1967 comprehensively altered the valuation procedures that had previously accompanied an act of expropriation.[59] Prior to the amendment, the Constitution provided that the state could take private property solely by way of a judicial decree or by reason of public benefit as declared in an appropriate legislative act.[60] The revised language now reads:

> No one may be deprived of his property except by virtue of a general or special law authorizing expropriation for reasons of public utility or social interests.[61]

The apparent effect of this amendment is to remove expropriatory power from the province of the ordinary courts and subject it entirely to legislative discretion, which may now be exercised not only under the old standard of "public utility" but also in the furtherance of "social interests."[62]

The new constitutional provisions state that each piece of legislation supporting expropriation will set forth the methods of acquisition, enjoyment, and disposition of property in order to ensure its "social function" and "accessibility to all." In this particular context, the sweeping Agrarian Reform Law is a good example of the effect of the constitutional changes on valuation proceedings.[63] Basically, the law permits expropriation of all holdings of more than eighty-eight hectares for redistribution to qualified individuals and agrarian cooperatives. A state corporation established by earlier legislation,[64] the Agrarian Reform Corporation (CORA), was designated to handle all administrative matters relating to the reform. This corporation, within which the Agrarian Settlement Fund functions, was empowered to acquire agricultural lands by any of

[59] Ley No. 16,615, Diario Official Jan. 20, 1967.

[60] *See* Martel, *Chile* in EXPROPRIATION IN THE AMERICAS 81, 92 (A. Lowenfeld ed. 1971). *See also* Allison, *Recent Legal Developments in Latin America,* 2 INT'L LAWYER 286 (1968). Also of considerable interest is Valdes, *La Reforma Constitutional del Derecho de Propriedad,* REVISTA DE DERECHO PÚBLICO, July / Dec. 1966, at 95, 102–105.

[61] *See* note 39 *supra*.

[62] *See* note 60 *supra*.

[63] Ley No. 16,640, Diario Oficial July 28, 1967.

[64] Ley No. 15,020, Diario Oficial Nov. 27, 1962.

the following methods: (1) by bids for public auctions, (2) by direct private purchase, (3) by expropriation, and (4) by transfer from the government. The latest legislative enactment establishes expropriation as the predominant mode of acquiring land.[65]

Both agrarian reform acts contained provisions that established a system of specialized courts to resolve all legal disputes arising from the expropriations. A subsequently enacted decree enumerates the functions of the Agrarian Reform Tribunals.[66] The jurisdictional bases are: (1) that they function under the auspices of the Supreme Court of Chile and have both trial and appellate levels, (2) that they are charged with responsibility for adjudicating agrarian claims, and (3) that they are bound in their awards and judgments by the constitutional and legislative limits. Therefore, to the degree that governmental decrees and legislation vacillate, the jurisdictional and discretionary scope of the court does also. This factor may in certain instances lessen the predictability of the Chilean procedural scheme.

Article 42 of the Agrarian Reform Law provides that the compensation payable to owners of expropriated rural properties shall be equivalent to the assessed valuation in effect for purposes of the land tax, including any improvements not included in the valuation. The compensation is payable partly in cash and the remainder in Agrarian Reform bonds. Article 132 creates three classes of bonds, A, B, and C, whose periods of amortization are twenty-five, five, and thirty years respectively. Each class of bond is issued in two series; 70 percent in the first series, which is adjusted annually in accordance with increases in the consumer price index as determined by the Internal Revenue Service, and 30 percent in the second series, which is not subject to adjustment. Each class of bond bears a 3 percent annual interest rate and is guaranteed by the State. The proportion of cash to bond payment is directly linked to the state in which the expropriated rural property is found. For example, in the case of abandoned property, 1 percent is payable in cash; if the land is poorly exploited, 3 to 5 percent in cash; the remainder in both cases is payable in thirty-year Class C bonds. In most cases, 10 percent is paid in cash, the remainder in twenty-five-year Class A bonds.

Under the Agrarian Reform Law, the actual preliminary valuation is to be made by a specialized technical body within the CORA.[67] This is consistent with the notion that the expropriating

---

[65] *See* note 63 *supra.*

[66] *See* Diario Oficial Oct. 25, 1967.

[67] Alicia Riesco U., 65 Rev. Der. Juris., Sec. I, at 378 (1968).

authority will make a provisional determination of the amount of compensation.[68] Any party affected by the valuation then has thirty days within which to appeal the determination to the Provincial Agrarian Tribunal in order to test the valuation of improvements since the last tax assessment.[69] It appears however, that the appeal bears only on depreciation, as the tax basis remains unchallenged in this instance.

D. THE ARGENTINE VALUATION PROCESS

Special procedural steps also must be followed in Argentina.[70] Under the Argentine Constitution, indemnification ultimately will be determined by a court of law if the amount is contested.[71] This does not, however, preclude an out-of-court settlement between the property owner and the expropriating authority. Yet, as a practical matter, this manner of settlement is very seldom used, principally because the amount of recovery in such settlements is limited to the assessed tax value plus 30 percent, a sum often only 50 percent of the actual value. In most cases, absent such an accord, the expropriating authority is obliged under the general law of expropriation[72] to initiate proceedings in the Federal Court of the First Instance of the appropriate district.[73] As an aid to the Federal Court, the permanent Argentine Assessment Tribunal[74] sits in Buenos Aires to advise the Federal judges as to the proper methods and amounts of valuation. Upon request from the judge who is to rule on the compensation, the Tribunal must reach a decision within ninety days as to the valuation of the expropriated property.[75] The owner is, of course, notified during the interim that he may appoint a representative to participate in the Tribunal's deliberations, during

[68] *See* note 22 *supra.*

[69] Ley No. 16,640 art. 42 (1967).

[70] Dawson, *Panel: The Taking of Property: Evaluation of Damages,* 62 PROCEEDINGS AM. SOC'Y INT'L L. 39–40 (1968).

[71] Lugui, *supra* note 14, at 1026.

[72] Ley No. 13,264, Boletín Oficial Dec. 22, 1948. Real property may also be taken under Ley No. 14,392, Boletín Oficial Jan. 10, 1955, the purpose of which is to promote rural settlement and land reform.

[73] Law and Judicial Systems of Nations, Argentina 6 (1968).

[74] This Tribunal, which is more an administrative body than a court, was established as a technical body to render decisions in assessments of valuation. The Tribunal is composed of ten permanent members plus one member appointed by the property owner and one by the expropriating agency. Gordillo, *Argentina* in EXPROPRIATION IN THE AMERICAS 11, 38 (A. Lowenfeld, ed. 1971). Western Telegraph Co. Ltd. v. Klein, Nelly y otros, 121 LA LEY 546 (1966).

[75] Ley No. 13,264.

which time competent evidence may be received as to the actual value of the property. Although the final decision of the Federal Court is not as a matter of course required to be based upon the advice from the Tribunal, its opinion on the matter is nearly always accepted. The judge has authority to decide the issue of valuation based on the record before him and the findings of the Tribunal. The trial court is prohibited from hearing expert testimony as to value for the simple reason that that function is exercised by the Assessment Tribunal.[76] So in essence, the conclusions of the Tribunal are of a binding character. Nevertheless, where there is sufficient reason to believe that the conclusions are in error, the trial court may disregard them.[77] As indicated, in Argentina the determination of compensation in expropriatory situations is a question to be settled exclusively by the judiciary.[78] And unlike the procedural system of valuation in Mexico, the rulings of the Federal Courts may be challenged through the appellate process.[79]

IV. DOMESTIC VALUATION TECHNIQUES

The role of the judiciary in resolving issues of valuation in common law nations differs radically from that in the countries sur-

---

[76] Nación Argentina v. Dominquez y Cia, 248 FALLOS 146 (1960).

[77] In order to be ignored, the report must have been rendered on grounds other than those authorized by the Supreme Court. Ricaurte Immobilaria v. Municipalidad de la Capital, 121 LA LEY 659 (1966); Gasi, S.A. v. Municipalidad de la Capital, 121 LA LEY 538 (1966); Terzolo v. Municipalidad de la Capital, 122 LA LEY 529 (1966).

[78] Provincia de Entre Rios v. Talaganis de Talaselis, 106 LA LEY 611 (1962). *See also* Canasi, *La Prescripción de la Acción de Retrocesión en la Expropiación Pública,* 122 LA LEY 430 (1966). The author points out that "[t]o establish the institution of expropriation necessitates the intervention of three State powers: the Legislative Power to declare through law the necessity of the work and its benefit; the Judicial Power to determine the amount of indemnification that should be given to the owner; and the Executive Power in order that through its various organs the act is executed." *Id.* at 441.

[79] *See* note 73 *supra*. The national appellate court system was established by Law No. 13,998 of Oct. 6, 1950, as later confirmed by Decree-Law 1285 of Feb. 4, 1958, arts. 52–54. These tribunals sit *en banc* for certain administrative matters, and the jurisdiction of these courts comprehends: cases coming through the appellate process; cases where the nation is a direct party; cases in which value in conflict exceeds a specified amount; cases based on denial of justice in lower courts (this is a probable claim in valuation proceedings); review of extradition claims of foreign nations; admiralty cases involving capture or embargo in times of war, nationality of vessels and salvage cases; and matters related to letters, patents, and other papers.

veyed. The Anglo-American systems permit the judiciary considerable discretion in developing and shaping standards applicable to the resolution of compensable claims.[80] The courts also have been free to fashion criteria against which the acceptability of evidence of value is weighed. This substantial judicial power is attributable perhaps to the lack of constitutional provisions that speak directly to property valuation in eminent domain actions, or perhaps to the vagueness of relevant common law practices. In Latin America, however, constitutional provisions governing expropriations, and legislative enactments that implement the state's expropriatory power, have placed severe limitations on the court's jurisdiction in valuation proceedings.[81] Nevertheless, there are a variety of valuation rules found in the municipal law of the countries surveyed.

A. General Valuation Methods

Two basic technical approaches can be used to ascertain the value of real property. One is based on the extrinsic, the other on the intrinsic value of the affected property.[82] Whatever the legal standards for proof of valuation are, appraisers utilize their own specialized techniques to determine the value of expropriated property. In this regard, the Argentine Supreme Court has indicated that it is impossible to determine the value of a given property without referring to technical standards that are not necessarily governed by legal rules or procedures. Consequently, the courts in Argentina customarily permit appraisers to utilize the following techniques in calculating real property valuation.[83]

---

[80] Evidence of this fact can be found in Smith, *supra* note 46, at 142–67. The evidentiary standards have been determined by judicial rather than legislative limit in Canada, England, and the United States.

[81] *See, e.g.,* the case of Vicente Alamos I., 65 Rev. Der. Juris., Sec. I, at 2 (1968). The fifth paragraph of the newly adopted Chilean constitutional revision:
"deprives the parties of the power to arrive at a process which they esteem to be conducive to accredit the effective value of the expropriated good and the tribunal to fix the amount of indemnification in excess of the limits preestablished by the law, whatever the conclusion which could lead to this excessive value." Constitution art. 10 (10) .

[82] *See* E. Fitte & A. Cervini, Antecedentes para el Estudio de Normas para Tasaciones Urbanos en Capital Federal 4, 8 (2d ed. 1946) ; 1 J. Canasi, Tratado Teórico Práctico de la Expropriación Pública 109 (1967) ; E. Lapa, *supra* note 30, at 138–40 (1968) .

[83] 242 Fallos 151 (1958) .

1. Extrinsic Valuation

The extrinsic valuation scheme[84] may employ any one or a combination of four general tests of value. The first, the direct or comparative method, results from an evaluation by comparison of critical factors. The property to be taken is priced by comparing its characteristics with those of the surrounding property of similar quality and age.[85] The market value may or may not affect this valuation, for the sales in that area and at that time are to be considered as only one of several factors.[86] The comparative values of adjoining land, though not for sale, are also relevant. In Argentina, for example, if the value of adjacent land has been fixed as a result of expropriation proceedings, that valuation typically will serve as a comparative basis for fixing compensation for the land in question.[87] For the purposes of the appraisal, the value of the land is calculated separately from that of the buildings.[88]

Since this method depends upon information that must be taken from official records pertaining to sales of land and taxes, the information may be misleading because individuals may list fictitious sales prices in order to evade payment of higher taxes.[89] Moreover, this method does not take into account circumstances that may tend to distort the worth of the property. This method could have a certain double-edged effect if the property ultimately is expropriated and the valuation is based upon the owner's recordation at the time of purchase.

The second method, indirect valuation, applies the principle of capitalization to properties that are capable of generating income through rents or leases.[90] Here, the focal point of inquiry is the

[84] The extrinsic method enables the appraiser to reach a value for the property which is often referred to as the objective value of the property. The Argentine Expropriation Law sets for the following principle:
"Compensation shall only comprehend the *objective value* of the property and those damages that are a direct and immediate consequence of the expropriation" [emphasis added]. Ley No. 13,264, art. 11.
See also Cirelo Juan Zanola v. Nación Argentina, 253 FALLOS 307 (1962).

[85] E. FITTE & A. CERVINI, *supra* note 82, at 4.

[86] E. LAPA, ESTUDIO DEL TÍTULO DE PROPRIEDAD / LA TASACIÓN DE INMUEBLES 138 (1968). *See also* Nación Argentina v. Santo Capello, 247 FALLOS 545 (1960).

[87] Nación Argentina v. Compta, 246 FALLOS 208 (1960).

[88] E. LAPA, note 86 *supra*.

[89] *Id.* at 139.

[90] Capitalization is one of the components of the concept of "fair value" that grew out of the case of Smyth v. Ames, 169 U.S. 466 (1898), which has been ac-

capacity of the property to produce income. Factors such as the calculation of rent received over a twelve-month period, the amount of general expenditures, and the sum of depreciation[91] are relevant to this inquiry. The net rent capitalized, once determined, is regarded as indicative of the property's value. In cases where the state can acquire the property through negotiation and ultimate purchase, the Mexican practice includes the use of the capitalized value method based on the productivity of the property.[92] This method has obvious defects. A property's ability to produce income does not always reflect value. This is especially true in many Latin American countries where chronic inflation and frequent monetary devaluation militate against stable real property valuation.[93]

The third method is denominated as empiric.[94] This method employs statistical investigations as to comparative values and intrinsic / extrinsic observations as to worth. Moreover, the experience of the appraiser affects the objective appreciation of value in this method. One of the strengths of the empiric approach, from a free market point of view, is that it permits consideration of the effects of present market values under the operation of supply and demand.[95] To the extent that the method is based upon records made after sale, it will suffer from the same infirmities of misrepresentation as the direct valuation approach.

---

cepted to a certain degree by the Argentine courts as an accurate measure of the value of real property used for business purposes. Oddly, the *Smyth* case was not an expropriate case but rather one which involved rate regulation. In *Smyth* the Supreme Court stated that the following criteria could be used to value the properties in question: (1) the original cost of construction, (2) the amounts expended for capital improvements, (3) the amount and market value of stocks and bonds, (4) the present cost of construction, and (5) the probable earning capacity of the properties.

[91] *See* note 87 *supra.*

[92] Trevino, *Mexico,* in Expropriation in the Americas 113, 144–45 (A. Lowenfeld ed. 1971).

[93] Though for years the Argentine courts rejected evidence of monetary devaluation as nonprobative of value, the reasoning of Pinto Beltras v. Empresa Nacional de Energia, 122 La Ley 943 (1966) set forth by the Federal Court in Tucuman was accepted by the Argentine Supreme Court the following year. In Iturreria v. Gobierno Nacional, 268 Fallos 340 (1967), the Supreme Court allowed monetary devaluation to be taken into account to increase the sum of compensation from m$n10,407,000 to m$n12,488,400. That decision set aside precedents of twenty years' standing which had held that fluctuations in monetary values were not compensable, see 209 Fallos 333 (1947).

[94] *Supra* note 29, at 6.

[95] E. Lapa, note 86 *supra,* at 139. In the case of widespread agrarian reform however, this strength would be dissipated as there would be no market for land subject to imminent expropriation.

Lastly, the appraiser may use a mixed method of valuation. This technique enables the value of the property to be determined upon a base arrived at by combining the best features of the methods explained above. The general goal of this approach therefore is to diminish the possibilities of error and to increase the probability of arriving at an ideal value.[96]

2. Intrinsic Valuation

The second basic approach exemplifies an attempt to determine the intrinsic value of the affected property. This technique consists of a calculation founded upon the value of the real property, which is attained by a comparative method or by *venal* value,[97] and the value of the buildings, assessed according to their actual state.[98] From this value is deducted a sum representing the depreciation for age. Some criticism has been leveled at this technique as it allegedly reflects foreign standards.[99]

B. TECHNICAL ASPECTS OF EVALUATION PROCEDURES

1. Land

With regard to land itself, a valuation may take into consideration the location of the property in relation to, among other things: proximity to business centers and means of communication; type, class, number, and utilization of nearby highways; neighboring businesses and industry; parks and other places for recreation; schools and cultural centers.[100] Each of these factors, and of course their totality, can influence favorably the economic value or price of the land.

The particular location of land, its uniqueness, and other factors peculiar to the individual plot also affect value. Moreover, the location of the lot within a block or general area is significant with respect to its relation to intersections, transportation routes, or adja-

---

[96] *See* note 29 *supra.*

[97] The venal value represents an attempt to determine value as to marketability.

[98] E. LAPA, *supra* note 86, at 8.

[99] *Id.*

[100] Rocca, *Reglas en La Tasación Judicial de Inmuebles,* 114 LA LEY 651, 655 (1964) .

cent points of traffic.[101] If land is expropriated for the construction
of a highway, adjacent property or property owned by the same
person, but not taken, may increase in value. Traditionally, Chilean practice in expropriation cases involving public construction
activity has been to ignore the increase in property value stemming
from the taking.[102] Recent Chilean legislation, however, has included provisions that permit a setoff between the increase in the
worth of the remaining land and the amount of compensation. The
1960 Construction and Urbanization Law[103] states that "whenever
property acquires greater value in consequence of its partial expropriation, such increase in value of the part not expropriated shall
be deducted from the compensation payable for the expropriated
part." For valuation purposes, the Argentine practice is to treat the
expropriated land as though it had not been the object of an expropriation.[104] Therefore, the value of the property theoretically is not
affected by the taking.

Of course, the measurements of the land are important, particularly the amount of footage that abuts various streets and highways.[105] The form of the land, such as regularity of dimension, may
also aid a positive valuation. The quality of the land, including
potential uses and favorable characteristics of subsoil, slope level,
and altitude in relation to adjoining pieces, may bear favorably
on the valuation.[106] The existence of sanitation and water facilities
on the property is also meaningful in assessing value. To the ex-

---

[101] *Id.*

[102] CÓDIGO DE PROCEDIMIENTO CIVIL art. 917.

[103] Ley de Construcción y Urbanización, DFL 192 of March 25, 1960, Boletín
Oficial Apr. 1, 1960. The provision of the law appears to be an attempt to eliminate windfall benefits to the property owner. The concept's constitutionality has
been upheld by the Chilean Supreme Court: "In order to determine the value
required to be paid for expropriation for a highway it is appropriate to reduce
the sum representing the value of the expropriated land by an amount corresponding to the increase in value acquired by the land remaining in the
hands of the expropriated party which is attributable to the purpose for which
the expropriation took place." Abraham Villanova Machado v. State (Fisco),
48 REV. DER. JURIS., Sec. I, at 418 (1950).

[104] Ley No. 13, 264 art. 11 (1948). *But see* Nación Argentina v. Salvador de
Rosa, 242 FALLOS 11 (1958), where the Supreme Court upheld a compensation
award against the challenge that the lower court permitted the use of the increase in value resulting from the announcement of expropriation in making its
judgment.

[105] *See* Ricaurte Inmobilaria v. Municipalidad de la Capital, 121 LA LEY 659
(1966), which holds that the expropriator is required to pay for the property
as determined by the exact measurement of its dimensions.

[106] *See* note 100 *supra*.

tent that these characteristics are extant, the value of the land increases.

The physical endowment and the availability of certain conveniences on a piece of land can also affirmatively increase its worth. For instance, the presence of gardens, shade or fruit trees, drainage improvements, gas, electricity, and telephone connections produces an increase in value.[107]

2. Buildings

As previously noted, buildings generally are evaluated as a separate yet complementary part of the whole property.[108] This distinction serves a useful purpose since, in terms of valuation, there are inherent differences between the land and the quality of the building situated upon the lot.

The first point of consideration is the extent to which the building has been constructed at the moment of expropriation. Each step of the construction can be assigned a statistical percentage of the projected total value which can represent approximate value: preparation of the terrain, excavation, and leveling, 1.5%; fulfillment of general tasks such as acquiring insurance and adherence to local regulations, 2.5%; setting of foundations and general structures, 20%; placement of superstructures and roof, 15%; installation of plumbing and kitchen fixtures, electrical wiring, 5%; completion of sewage system and waterline connections, 10%; installations, 5%; walls, 10%; floors, 10%; woodwork and metalwork, 10%; paint, glass, and terminations, 5%; other general finishing work, 6%.[109]

The quality of the construction also may be indicative of certain inherent values. It is apparent that a building's value may vary depending on its classification as to type or quality of construction. The Argentine system of valuation has established a specific scale against which the quality of construction may be measured and integrated into the appraised value. This rather general classification encompasses five grades of construction, each of which is a result of a judgment as to quality: luxury, high quality, economy, regular, and low quality.[110] It is obvious, however, that with such a

[107] *Id.*
[108] *See* note 86 *supra.*
[109] *See supra* note 100, at 658.
[110] *Id.*

system there exist intermediate types and considerable overlap between categories.

Some attention is also given to the age of the building.[111] This factor works against the possibility of appreciation of the building's value. The building is assigned an arbitrary life. Each year the value of the building is reduced by a computed percentage. Similar to depreciation, this deduction diminishes the value of the property in the final appraisal. Nevertheless, the Latin American systems adhere to this procedure.[112] However, the value of the building never reaches zero. Although this procedure may appear economically unproductive, the age of the building is critical to its value—at least to the extent that age parallels deterioration of the edifice. Under certain circumstances, specifically in cases of expropriations of property for the construction of streets, parks, or public buildings, if the affected building is deemed in poor condition, the Chilean valuation will include only the value of the land; no compensation will be allowed for the demolished building.[113]

Perhaps the age coefficient has greater significance when tied to another factor, the status of the building as regarding separability. This particular factor is evaluated in terms of the following categories: those buildings which have not suffered deterioriation and do not need repairs; those which require nonessential repairs; those which need simple repairs that cannot be postponed without causing more serious damage; those which require important repairs; and those buildings which are practically without value unless fundamental, costly, and urgent repairs are made.[114]

Another factor often considered in the case of rental property is the ability of the building to produce income. If the building is old, but of excellent construction, and located in the central zones of a city, the rentability of the property may completely negate the

[111] *Id.* at 659. *See also* Velasco, note 54 *supra,* for a discussion of the constitutional implications of these precepts in Mexico; A. ROJAS, *supra* note 49, at 52. A recent Argentine case held that the value of a building may be diminished by the factor of obsolescence but that if this factor is used one cannot discount the value again based upon the age. Gorostiague v. Gobierno Nacional, 127 LA LEY 883 (1967).

[112] *Id.*

[113] Ley General de Construcción y Urbanización, as amended (1963). Because Chile does not have a general expropriation law, the valuation of properties not covered by recent constitutional changes will be carried out under the provisions of Articles 915–25 of the CÓDIGO DE PROCEDIMIENTO CIVIL.

[114] *See* Rocca, *supra* note 100, at 659. The loss of value due to the deterioration of the property will be set by local courts in Chile and Mexico.

decrease in value brought about by the age of the building.[115] As noted, the critical factor here is the location of the building, which must be an area where there is possibility for leasing or renting.[116] The more favorable the location, the higher will be the value of the property.

The sum of these diverse values and factors will lead to a determination of the total value of the property, thus combining the value of the land and the buildings. The resulting combined value will then constitute the figure that will be presented by the expert appraiser for registration or to the judge, who will resolve the issue based upon the jurisprudence previously mentioned.[117] Yet it is notable that the opinions of independent appraisers are only an approximation of true value and that a judge is, in some instances, relatively free to accept or reject the valuation and / or adjust it to meet the demands of justice within the limits placed upon him by legislative acts or constitutional provisions.[118]

C. Comparative Value Base

The valuation techniques in Argentina clearly involve an appraisal based upon a comparative analysis which may include more

[115] *Id.* at 660; *see* text accompanying note 125 *infra.* But in event of a taking, the Argentine Expropriation Law provides that loss of future profits will not figure in the compensation. Ley No. 13,264, art. 2.

[116] Where property is subject to a lease, the Argentine system of valuation normally considers the worth or detriment that lease has to the property in question by considering the *coeficiente de disponibilidad.* However, the fact that the property is encumbered by a lease will not be considered in a compensation judgment for expropriation. Ortiz v. Municipalidad de la Capital, 106 LA LEY 805 (1962). But under the Mexican Civil Code if the contract for a lease is rescinded by expropriation, both the owner and lessee are to be compensated by law for moving costs, new rent if it varies from the contract rent, and lost income. CÓDIGO CIVIL art. 2410.

[117] *See* note 115 *supra.*

[118] In cases arising under the reach of agrarian reform in Chile and Mexico, this judicial independence has as its general limit the tax value if it has been recorded. Even where this value is not registered or where the valuation is being performed to establish the increase or diminution in value due to improvements or demerits, the courts are still subject to the appraisals made by the experts appointed by the court. Yet because Chile has no general expropriation law, the general procedures of valuation for eminent domain proceedings are located in the Civil Code. Under those rules the judge is not bound by the appraisals of the experts. CÓDIGO DE PROCEDIMIENTO art. 918. *See* notes 128–130 *infra.*

than the value of the property for tax purposes. Such a valuation utilizes a comparative process which considers the current value and market offers, as well as the valuation of immovables for purposes of collecting taxes.[119] Although this more expansive method of valuation is employed principally in Argentina, it has been used from time to time to value expropriated property in Mexico and Chile when either improvements have been made or no tax value exists. For such purposes the value is determined at the time the expropriation was ordered.[120] If the tax value is not recorded, it is possible to circumvent the constitutional restraints that limit the valuation to tax value. The Mexican system clearly provides for a valuation independent of the records on the request of either party. Once established, an alternative appraisal may become the basis of a totally new valuation. The limits of the Chilean agrarian reform method of valuation are adhered to more rigorously because the tax valuation basis is the mode for establishing worth, whether or not it is presently recorded.[121] Yet for nonagrarian expropriations, other factors will be given consideration.

D. The Preeminence of the Tax Value Basis

Expert appraisers and the courts most often are aided in valuation procedures by referring to official or public registers, to protocols prepared by court clerks, lawyers, or notaries, to records of judicial sales, to current sales records, to information supplied by banks, and to individual sales in the area.

It is no surprise, therefore, that domestic valuation schemes in Argentina, Chile, and Mexico fundamentally emphasize the tax value of the property that is subject to expropriation.[122] In general,

---

[119] R. Galarce & A. Matienzo, La Expropriación en El Código Civil Argentino 67–68 (1937) ; *see also* Brisk, *Tax Evaluation as a Measure of Compensation for Expropriated Property in Argentina, Columbia and Guatemala,* 19 N.Y.U. Intra. L. Rev. 52 (1964) .

[120] J. Canasi, El Justiprecio en la Expropriación Pública 160 (1952) .

[121] *See* note 81 *supra.*

[122] Article 9 of the Argentine Law No. 14,392 (1955) states that fiscal value is but one of several elements to be considered. On the other hand, the Chilean Agrarian Reform Law recited that

"[t]he expropriating entity will make a provisional determination of the indemnification, taking into account the valuation made for the purpose of territorial contribution. . . ." Ley No. 16,640 (1967) .

Likewise, the Mexican Law of Expropriation establishes in Article 10 that "[t]he price which is fixed as the indemnification for the item expropriated will

the value of the property recorded on the tax registers is the basis for a determination of the amount of indemnification that will be paid to the expropriated owner.[123] Although some assert that recorded tax value is indicative of market value based on the contemporary supply and demand function,[124] it is notable that before the constitutional changes in Chile, there was an obvious disparity between the figures on the records and those upon which the courts predicated their awards.[125]

Because the recently enacted amendments to the Chilean Constitution provide that expropriation legislation establish the methods and limits of valuation for taken properties, no expropriatory agency may award compensation in excess of the prescribed limits;[126] to do so would be ultra vires and unconstitutional. In addition, if the legislation specifies the exclusive use of the tax value method, the courts are bound by that determination. Consequently, the courts, in such cases, may be restrained in the use of evidence that is probative of value. One explanation for this action is that the Chilean authorities felt the previous methods of valuation involved contentious proceedings that were cumbersome and frequently resulted in awards of excessive compensation. Thus, the legislature imposed substantial limits on the judiciary's freedom of action for the sake of expediency and accuracy.[127] Despite some general differences, the Mexican system functions similarly to that in Chile.

In Mexico and Chile, any appreciation in real property value attributable to improvements exceeding that recorded in the tax registers after the last fiscal valuation may be considered in determining the amount of payable compensation.[128] Such appreciations may be assessed either by experts or the courts. Under the

---

be based upon the amount which represents its fiscal value as found in the tax collection offices, whether this value has been manifested by the property owner or simply accepted by him in a tacit manner by paying the contribution affixed upon this base."

[123] See note 122 *supra.*

[124] H. VILLALOBOS, LA EXPROPRIACIÓN Y SU PROCEDIMIENTO 68 (1957).

[125] *See* Valdes, *La reforma constitutional de derecho de propriedad,* REVISTA DE DERECHO PÚBLICO Nos. 5–6, at 104 (1966); *but see* Allison, *Recent Legal Developments in Latin America,* 2 INT'L LAWYER 286 (1968). Since commercial values are usually considerably greater than assessed values, the fourth clause of the Chilean constitutional revision, which sets the property valuation for tax purposes as the base of compensation, places the property owner at some disadvantage.

[126] *See* note 81 *supra.*

[127] Valdes, note 125 *supra.*

[128] Ley No. 16,615 art. 10(10) (1967); Ley de Expropriación (Mexico) art. 10 (1936).

expropriation law currently in force in Argentina, if the parties agree to an out-of-court settlement, then the agreed compensation cannot exceed 30 percent of the tax value in effect at that time.[129] Yet there is some indication that this percentage limit is not strictly adhered to, as the tax value is only one of several techniques to determine value. In fact, Argentine courts have recognized that tax value is not a fair basis for determining the value of property.[130] Nevertheless, the tax basis plus 30 percent does serve as the touchstone for valuation by the Assessment Tribunal.

A loss of value occasioned by any one of several events, such as storm damage, fire, or structural collapse, necessarily causes a diminution in the value of the property. Where the fiscal valuation limit is known and used, the resulting decrease in value may be appraised and considered in the judgment.[131] This procedure may be accomplished by either the appraisers or the courts.

Some flaws in the tax value basis are readily apparent; others are more subtle. Perusal of the laws governing registration of the fiscal value of property reveals some interesting data. In Chile, the owners of property are permitted to play a rather active role in the fiscal valuation process.[132] They are required by law to prepare an estimate of the value of their holdings as a foundation for a general reassessment for tax records. Yet it is highly questionable, for obvious reasons, whether the owners would submit a value which could seriously be considered as the full or real value of the property. Using the information given them, the fiscal appraisers would calculate the basic tax value of the property by taking into account such things as measurements, location, and selling price during the last few years. Theoretically, by using this technique, the value ultimately registered in the tax office would be regarded as an accurate representation of what the property would bring if sold in a competitive market. Yet when compared with the amounts awarded by earlier judicial determinations, the use of this theoretical or ideal value lacks credibility. For example, court awards before the enactment of the Chilean Agrarian Reform Law were

129 Ley No. 13,264 art. 13. However, the out-of-court settlement has fallen into general disuse. *See also* Brisk, *supra* note 119, at 56. Consider also Adminstración General de Transportes de Buenos Aires v. Corral y Saavedra, 122 LA LEY 657 (1966), which held that the courts are not bound to use the method of valuation used by the expropriator in its deliberations.

130 Banco de la Nación Argentina v. Sorbet, 248 FALLOS 452 (1960).

131 *See* note 128 *supra*.

132 *Id. See also* Ley No. 15,021, Diario Oficial Nov. 16, 1962, which required taxpayers to prepare a statement estimating the value of the property.

three or four times those of the recorded fiscal values.[133] Neverthe-less, the fiscal value method may very well be highly reliable as a guaranteed minimal standard of valuation for expropriated real property, especially where national interests outweigh the rights of individuals in economic reform situations.

E. Valuation Formulas for Business

When the object of an expropriation is a manufacturing plant, public utility, mine, church, school, or building under construc-tion,[134] neither the tax value nor comparative market value tests can be applied with certainty.[135] In fact, in such instances the market value test, as normally applied, is inapplicable because the target of the expropriation is not subject to constant market move-ment. Accordingly, comparative market valuation fails here as a reliable means of ascertaining worth. Consequently, an alternative method of determining the value of the expropriated property must be used. In Argentina, Chile, and other Latin American states, this dilemma has been resolved by appropriate legislative measures designed to govern the valuation process.[136] There are various reasons underlying resort to a legislative solution.[137] First, it was felt that valuation *stricto sensu*, with its ample interplay between appraisers, judges, and public officials, tended to distort

[133] 3 R. Bielsa, Derecho Administrativo 434 (1939). *See also* Luz Bungas y Robles, 3 S.J.F. 417 (1918), in which the Mexican Supreme Court commented on the disparity between the fiscal value, which the parties who sought an ex-propriation of land proposed to pay, and the actual value by stating that there was a wide gap between them because "the parties interested in the formation of such a company obtain a universal profit due to the fact that the valuation of the land in accordance with the fiscal value test is worth eight centavos per meter, and they can sell it immediately for four pesos per meter."

[134] *See* text accompanying note 109 *supra*.

[135] This notion is not new, nor is it startling. Various Anglo-American authors and courts have recognized this fact. *See generally* A. Jahr, Law of Eminent Domain: Valuation and Procedure 116–22 (1953).

[136] *See* note 60 *supra*. *See also* Ley No. 5708 de la Provincia de Buenos Aires, art. 16, 12 Anuario de Legislación Argentina B1296 (1952). Article 4 of the Bolivian Decree nationalizing Gulf Oil Company establishes a commission which "with the technical advice that it may require, will establish the amount, conditions and terms of the corresponding indemnity." English text of Decree as reprinted in 8 Int'l Legal Materials 1163–64 (1969). For a discussion of ex-propriation of industries in Uruguay, see Prat, *Expropriación de empresas,* 19 Revista de la Facultad de Derecho y Ciencias Sociales 409 (1968).

[137] *See generally* J. Oyhanarte, La Expropriación y los Servicios Públicos 79 (1957).

the amount of recoveries.[138] A legislatively prescribed valuation method would substantially reduce the incidence of excessive awards and help assure impartial judgments. Second, the technicalities attending the determination of value needed simplification. Third, a legislative valuation rule would also deter the use of deceptive practices by affected parties. Finally, the seriousness and frequency of monetary fluctuations were cited as reasons for adopting this particular method.

1. Capacity to Produce Versus Cost of Investment

An early Argentine case, *Ferrocarril de Entre Rios v. Gobierno de la Nación,* declared that: "The value of property is not that which has been invested in it. . . . The worth of a property is principally linked to its production or its ability to produce."[139]

The valuation test adopted in that case basically was one of going concern as it had been articulated in the United States.[140] The adoption of this particular method indicated the court's desire for a valuation technique which would vest the courts with considerable discretion. This method envisions two alternative approaches to determining value: first, a valuation according to the relative power of the enterprise to earn; and, second, a valuation based on an analysis made by considering all concurrent business factors.[141] Subsequent expropriation laws of Argentine provinces, which have dealt particularly with public service activities, have abandoned this technique completely. For example, Article 16 of Law No. 5708 of the Province of Buenos Aires supplanted the going concern test with the following formula: cost of investment less amortization and any profits deemed to be excessive.[142] This formula is

---

[138] P. VERNENGO, NATURALEZA DE LA EXPROPRIACIÓN 48–58 (1959); Valdes, *supra* note 60, at 104.

[139] 12 LA LEY 18 (1918). In that case, the Supreme Court decision set aside the method of valuation set by Law No. 6,341, amount of capital investment plus 20 percent, in favor of the ability to produce income test. *But see* Nación Argentina v. S.R.I. Astilleros Tigre, 259 FALLOS 277 (1964). The dissent of Boggero in that decision alludes to the fact that the majority refused to consider or alter the sum fixed as compensation or to accept by implication the going concern value as method of valuation.

[140] *See* note 90 *supra.*

[141] J. OYHANARTE, *supra* note 137, at 73–123.

[142] Excessive profits are defined by Argentine law as profits obtained from commerce, mining, industry, agriculture, or stock raising that exceed 12 percent of the capital and free reserves in a tax year. *But see* Provincia de Buenos Aires

premised upon the historic cost of the physical facilities and the time of acquisition. Moreover, at times a formula of prudent subsequent investments has also been taken into account.[143] This method takes into consideration the monetary sacrifice that the owner has incurred in an attempt to establish and operate the entity. In other words, those investments which are destined for use by the public service are favorably considered; those investments which are deemed superfluous, unnecessary, or exaggerated are deducted, thereby minimizing the amount of recovery. Under applicable legislation, courts generally have balked at accepting the going concern test for measuring the amount of compensation because it is too speculative.[144] Nevertheless, several lower federal and provincial courts have held that going concern value is an acceptable standard of valuation, especially when a public service entity is involved.[145]

2. Loss of Profits

The Argentine Supreme Court has refused to allow recovery for hypothetical future profits on the basis that such recoveries are excluded under the rubric of going concern value.[146] The parties may recover only the value of the taken assets and damages that flow directly from the expropriation. Therefore, under Argentine law, the lost profits due to business interruption by expropriation

---

v. Compania de Electricidad de Chivilocoy, S.A., 2 JURISPRUDENCIA ARGENTINA 26 (1967), which held that Article 16 was no longer the law under the Constitution of 1853. The test adopted was vague: the value of the assets at the moment of expropriation.

[143] An example of such a legislative formula is the Law of 1944 of the Province of Jujuy (Argentina), art. 41.

[144] Maipus Peinados, S.R.L. v. Empresa Nacional de Telecommunicaciones, 106 LA LEY 872 (1962).

[145] Betnaza v. Municipalidad de Coronel Suarez, Supreme Court of Buenos Aires, 4 JURISPRUDENCIA ARGENTINA 258 (1962); Provincia de Buenos Aires v. Compania de Electricidad de Dolores, S.A., Supreme Court of Buenos Aires, 6 JURISPRUDENCIA ARGENTINA 498 (1959). Several scholars have criticized the decisions of the Argentine Supreme Court that exclude from consideration the going concern value. "Within the doctrine and jurisprudence, the going concern value is something quite different from what is meant by unjust enrichment simply because the value of a "going concern" is a fact that can be ascertained. . . ." 1 J. CANASI, TRATADO TEÓRICO PRÁCTICO DE LA EXPROPRIACIÓN PÚBLICA 401 (1967).

[146] Nación Argentina v. Depieti, S.A., 256 FALLOS 232 (1963).

may not figure in the appraisal of indemnification.[147] Even though the value of the ongoing business may be considered an asset, Argentine courts consider any losses aside from those incurred as the result of the physical taking of the business as future profits and not compensable under the expropriation law.[148] This is not the case in Chile. Valuation under the General Law of Construction and Urbanization in theory may include not only the full value of land and buildings but also any damages resulting from lost profits from rents or business activities. Yet the compensation for the real property is limited to an amount not to exceed the declared tax value plus 10 percent.[149]

3. Good Will

In Chile, the intangible element of goodwill is essentially a factor which varies according to the changing economic position of a business and may or may not figure in its valuation. In the case of expropriation, indemnification should represent the value of the expropriated entity at the time of the taking. The Chilean Supreme Court has determined that if the value of good will is to be considered as part of the recovery, it must be determined with relative certainty.[150] When the good will value is deemed too speculative, it will be precluded from the amount of compensation.

On the other hand, Argentine courts totally reject the inclusion of good will in compensation awards, especially in cases pertaining to public service entities.[151] Even when the expropriation of private businesses is concerned, the value of good will is not considered on the theory that the good will is linked to the business, not to the particular property that has been taken. Good will in this instance is a value which depends on the existence of a future condition, the transfer of the business. As it is a value which tends to be associated with future expectations, it is classified with lost profits under Law No. 13,264 and therefore cannot be taken into account.[152]

---

[147] Article 2 of the Argentine Expropriation Law specifically states that future profits will not be taken into consideration in the valuation. *See also* Municipalidad de El Bolsar v. Albano, 106 LA LEY 234 (1962).

[148] Musso v. Nación Argentina, 242 FALLOS 254 (1958).

[149] Ley General de Construcción y Urbanización, *as amended* (1963).

[150] Case of Salvador Hess R., 65 REV. DER. JURIS., Sec. I, at 287 (1968).

[151] *See* note 147 *supra*.

[152] Musso v. Nación Argentina, 242 FALLOS 254 (1958).

4. Cost of Reproduction

One noted Argentine authority states that: "[t]he theory of fair value, with its consequent support by cost of reproduction, is erroneous in principle and defective in practice . . . [and] the cost of reproduction given to a property is not, nor can it be *per se,* a test of value."[153] This proposition rests on the notion that the purpose of valuation and subsequent compensation, while encompassing suffered damages, does not envision restoring the expropriated party to a position exactly equal to that before the expropriation occurred.[154] Therefore, cost of reproduction generally has no place in the determination of value in Argentina. However, in certain limited cases, the Argentine Supreme Court has permitted the use of cost of reproduction value in the measurement of compensation. In *Provincia de Buenos Aires v. Empresas Electricas de Bahía Blanca, S.A.,*[155] the court utilized the reproduction cost formula not on the basis of what it would cost the electric company to reproduce its assets, but rather on what it would cost the government to install a newspaper plant if it could not expropriate. In other words, the valuation was measured from the point of view of the benefit the local government would receive for not having to construct its own plant. The court permitted the use of the following alternative valuation formulas: either the present cost of reproduction to the government of that particular asset minus depreciation or the original cost of the plant to the company discounted by the depreciation, with the resulting figure to be adjusted by the variations in the cost of basic construction materials over the years. Moreover, in instances where it appears that the expropriated party will be unjustly enriched if the objective value of the property is used to measure compensation, the replacement cost will be used if it is the lowest value.[156]

5. Book Value

One of the most commonly used methods in Latin America for evaluating the assets of expropriated business property is by a

[153] 1 R. BIELSA, DERECHO ADMINISTRATIVO 426 *et seq.* (4th ed. 1939). *See also* J. CANASI, *supra* note 145, at 233.

[154] Gobierno Nacional v. Dumas, 47 LA LEY 865 (1947).

[155] 111 LA LEY 297 (1964).

[156] J. CANASI, note 120 *supra*, at 147.

book value test. In many instances, expropriatory legislation and executive decrees will actually stipulate the use of book value in calculating the amount of payable compensation. Chile is a good case in point. In 1967 and 1969 Kennecott and Anaconda respectively agreed to submit to President Eduardo Frei's "Chileanization" program whereby both concerns sold 51 percent of their equity interest in their subsidiaries to the Chilean Government and agreed to form mixed mining companies. In 1969 President Frei in a statement concerning the "Chileanization" agreements declared: "The purchase price of 51 percent will correspond to the book value of both companies, as set by the Copper Corporation and the Internal Revenue Department. . . . The book value on December 31, 1968, was approximately 197 million dollars."[157]

In 1971 President Salvador Allende, with the unanimous approval of the Chilean Congress, secured the passage of a constitutional amendment which authorized the nationalization of the Gran Mineria (the large copper mining sector). The apparent legal effect of the amendment was to repudiate and nullify the earlier "Chileanization" agreements and all legal obligations flowing from them. The amendment, which amends Article 10, Section 10, requires the Comptroller General of Chile to determine the maximum amount of compensation and to base his valuation exclusively on the book value of the companies' nationalized assets as of December 31, 1970. The amendment permits various deductions from book value, the most important of which are depreciations, damages to company assets, write-offs, amortizations, and excess profits (to be determined by the President). The Comptroller General calculated the book value of each affected enterprise from each concern's balance sheet. The basis of the calculation was the amount of paid-in capital and reserves, adding or subtracting profits or losses during the fiscal year, and deducting from this amount dividends actually paid or anticipated. In addition, the value of mineral deposits was not included in the amount of compensation since they are declared an inalienable part of the national patrimony. If the value of the mines was included in the companies' balance sheets, the Comptroller General deducted the amount indicated from the base book value.

This "adjusted" book value test certainly falls short of the "market value" and "going concern" valuation tests advocated by the copper companies and, in its application, arguably may fall below the minimum standard required by international law. The

[157] 8 INT'L LEGAL MATERIALS 1073 (1969).

Chilean government, in response to the companies' assertion that book value reflects an unduly low tax value of appraised assets, notes that the same concerns freely agreed to appraise their assets according to their own book values during the "Chileanization" negotiations. Despite the controversy over the appropriate test, it is clear that the Chilean government has ample precedent in support of its choice to continue using the book value method in expropriation cases.

The book value test is also utilized in the Argentine. For example, Law No. 5708 of the Province of Buenos Aires calls for a calculation based on the value of the investment less amortization and excess profits.

V. SUMMARY AND A PROPOSAL

Perhaps the major obstacle to fashioning an internationally acceptable valuation rule is the developing nation's insistence that foreign investors are not entitled to a higher standard of protection than local investors in wealth deprivation situations—a position generally unacceptable to most Western capital-exporting states.[158] The developing nation's position is articulated in the U.N. Declaration on Permanent Sovereignty over Natural Resources, which calls for appropriate compensation consistent with the municipal law of the expropriating state and complementary international law.[159] If a dispute arises over the amount of compensation, the Resolution would require aggrieved parties to seek redress within the legal system of the expropriating state and to exhaust all available remedies therein. The requirement of exhaustion of local remedies is a traditional principle of customary international law and encourages the settlement of investment disputes on the local level, rather than in the international arena. Although the Resolution cannot be regarded as authoritative or legally binding,[160] it provides a

[158] The Calvo Doctrine embraces two fundamental issues: (1) that sovereign states, being free and independent, enjoy the right, on the basis of equality, to freedom from interference from other states, either through force or diplomacy, and (2) that aliens are not entitled to rights and privileges not accorded to nationals. Dawson, *International Law, National Tribunals and the Rights of Aliens: The Latin American Experience,* 21 VAND. L. REV. 712, 719 (1968). *See generally* D. SHEA, THE CALVO CLAUSE (1955).

[159] *See* note 11 *supra; see also* RESTATEMENT (SECOND) OF FOREIGN RELATIONS LAW OF THE UNITED STATES § 185, Reporters' Notes ¶ 2 (1965).

[160] *But see* Orrego, La Resolución 1803 de la Asamblea General de Las Naciones Unidas Sobre "Soberania Permanente Sobre Los Recursos Naturales,"

realistic frame of reference in the search for a viable international compensation and valuation standard.

Disagreement over the choice of a particular valuation method often lies at the heart of most compensation disputes. This in turn reflects the lack of agreement as to what international law does or should require in the valuation process. Clearly, the market value test advocated by developed nations is not internationally acceptable as a standard inasmuch as it works against the interest of underdeveloped countries that must resort to expropriation as a means of reasserting national control over their basic domestic resources. Although the market value test is desirable from the point of view of the deprived party, it is not always an adequate measure of value, especially in cases where manufacturing plants, mines, and public services belonging to foreign interests are the target of expropriation. Neither are the interests of the expropriating state met if an exceedingly high test for valuation is employed. If the claims for compensation are so staggering as to jeopardize the nation's goals, then other considerations should be brought to bear in the valuation settlement.[161] It is necessary that the interests of private parties must be subordinated to those of the state in expropriation cases. Yet by this reasoning abusive practices may ensue; but this need not be so. Factors such as the number of claims involved, the absolute and relative economic position of the depriving and claimant parties, the capacity to pay for or absorb the losses inflicted, the past contributions made to the local economy and profits relative to that contribution, and the present and long-term interests of the claimant in the development of the depriving state ought to be important factors in determining what should be allowed as the basis of valuation.[162]

---

note 11 *supra,* wherein the author argues that the Resolution is an expression of current international law and as such has juridical value. *Id.* at 69.

[161] To quote one of the members of the Mexican Supreme Court: "We must not conclude without reiterating that compensation is only an expression of the spirit of justice which inspires the laws, but not an indispensable condition of every expropriation or of all injury that may be suffered by private property. Compensation must always, in technical terms, be conditioned not to compensate 100 percent, but to serve as a means of regulating the equilibrium of economic forces, since compensation must, like property, fulfill a social function and must therefore be limited or restricted to what social needs and possibilities permit, lest economic disequilibria caused by free competition and liberal principles of property which do not recognize the mediating intervention of the State be emphasized or barred." Garza, *Las modalidales de la propriedad,* as cited in L. Mendita y Nunez, El Sistema Agrario Constitucional 73 (3d ed. 1966).

[162] Weston, 62 Am. Soc'y Int'l L. Proceedings 43–46 (1968).

In valuation disputes, foreign investors should display utmost sensitivity to the principle of the sovereign and "juridicial equality of states."[163] Correspondingly, expropriating states should provide foreign investors with the same procedural rights they guarantee their nationals so as to avoid claims of discriminatory treatment that could give rise to international repercussions. In this regard, the Latin American states' adherence to doctrines similar to those propounded by Calvo should not provide a legal justification for engaging in otherwise discriminatory and arbitrary actions against aliens.[164]

In most expropriation cases, political and economic considerations often dictate what industry or particular property will be taken and are determinative of the maximum amount of indemnity to be paid. The seemingly arbitrary nature of this decision-making process and the absence of uniform international standards in such cases have been sources of continuing frustration to foreign investors. As depicted, the domestic valuation procedures in Argentina, Chile, and Mexico are rather explicit and comprehensive. They do not meet, however, the high valuation standards used in the Anglo-American systems.

The principal thrust of a valuation standard is to counterbalance monetary loss suffered as a result of expropriation. An acceptable international standard should not impede a state from implementing programs to achieve greater distributive and social justice, nor should it prevent the recovery from foreign interests of key industries that generate scarce foreign exchange, or those otherwise essential to the state's economic welfare. The imposition of valuation criteria that are entirely disproportionate to the ability of the state to compensate or do not conform to prevalent municipal law standards would have such an adverse effect. It would appear, therefore, that the tax value base, though arguably inadequate at times, is an appropriate minimum standard in real property valuation. Indeed, in certain instances, the tax valuations could maximize recoveries when social reforms become so vast that market value no longer has relevance. This standard obviously could be exceeded in many cases due to the higher standards maintained by certain countries like Argentina in their domestic valuation schemes.

International experience indicates persuasively that inflexible

---

[163] *See* Report of the Special Latin American Coordinating Committee on the Consensus of Viña del Mar, 8 INT'L LEGAL MATERIALS 974, 977 (1969).

[164] *See* Metzger, *Property in International Law*, 50 VA. L. REV. 594, 598 (1964).

insistence on a standard which embodies a theoretical maximum is foolhardy. Adoption of the tax value basis would ensure a high degree of compliance, increase stability of expectation in the international investment community, and, at the same time, probably not deter the flow of beneficial foreign investment, on a more equitable basis, to the world's developing countries. Moreover, it would permit more investment disputes to be settled within domestic legal systems[165] and thereby contribute to the strengthening of the international economic and legal order.

[165] A subsidiary of American & Foreign Power Company was expropriated by an Argentine municipality in 1958, and a settlement was soon agreed to through the joint efforts of the national governments, with the valuation to be based upon a court decree which was handed down in 1961. The uniqueness of this decree lies in the fact that it was the product of a relatively independent judicial determination of a domestic court. Such instances provide an optimistic lesson for the future. *See* Major Instances of Expropriation of Property Belonging to U.S. Nationals Since World War II in the Report of the Senate Comm. on Foreign Relations on S. 2996, S. Rep. No. 1535, 87th Cong., 2d Sess., at 93 (1962) .

Contributors

Thomas F. Bergin is William Minor Lile Professor of Law at the University of Virginia.

Dale B. Furnish is Professor of Law at Arizona State University.

Robert K. Goldman is Assistant Dean and Assistant Professor of Law at the American University Law School.

Richard B. Lillich is Professor of Law at the University of Virginia and Director of the Procedural Aspects of International Law Institute.

Joseph S. McCosker is Senior Lecturer of Accounting at the University of Southern California.

Norman N. Mintz is Assistant Dean of the Graduate School of Arts and Sciences and Assistant Professor of Economics at Columbia University.

John M. Paxman is Law Clerk to the United States District Court of the Virgin Islands.

Index